D0165044

THRESHOLD

Cambridge Pre-GED Program
in
Interpreting Literature and the Arts

Jerry Howett

Library of Congress Cataloging-in-Publication Data

Howett, Jerry.
   Threshold : Cambridge pre-GED program in interpreting literature
and the arts / Jerry Howett.
      p.   cm.
   ISBN 0–13–111097–7 (pbk.)
   1. General educational development tests—Study guides.
2. Reading (Secondary)—Examinations, questions, etc.
3. Literature—Examinations, questions, etc.   4. Arts—Examinations,
questions, etc.   I. Title.
LB3060.33.G45H7   1993
373.12′62—dc20   92–5687
                                                                        CIP

Publisher: TINA B. CARVER
Executive Editor: JAMES W. BROWN
Editorial Supervisor: TIMOTHY A. FOOTE
Managing Editor: SYLVIA MOORE
Production Editors: SHIRLEY HINKAMP AND SHARI TORON
Pre-press Buyer: RAY KEATING
Manufacturing Buyer: LORI BULWIN
Scheduler: LESLIE COWARD
Interior designers: JANET SCHMID and JANET S. JOHNSTON
Cover coordinator: MARIANNE FRASCO
Cover designer: BRUCE KENSELAAR
Cover photo: STOCK IMAGERY
Photo researcher: JULIE SCARDIGLIA
Permissions: ELLEN DIAMOND

Copyright © 1993 by Pearson Education, Inc., publishing as Pearson Learning Group, 299 Jefferson Road, Parsippany, NJ 07054. All rights reserved. No part of this book may be reproduced or transmitted in any form or by any means, electronic, or mechanical, including photocopying, recording, or by any information storage and retrieval system, without permission in writing from the publisher. For information regarding permission(s), write to Rights and Permissions Department.

ISBN 0-13-111097-7
Printed in the United States of America

8 9 10 11 12   06 05 04 03 02

1-800-321-3106
www.pearsonlearning.com

CONTENTS

Property of FLCC
Adult Basic Education
PLEASE RETURN

ACKNOWLEDGMENTS

CAMBRIDGE Adult Education thanks the men and women enrolled in ABE and Pre-GED courses who read parts of the *Threshold* manuscripts and offered valuable advice to the programs' authors and editors.

We also thank the following consultants for their many contributions throughout the preparation of the *Threshold* Pre-GED programs.

Cecily Kramer Bodnar
Consultant, Adult Learning
Adult Literacy Services
Central School District
Greece, New York

Pamela S. Buchanan
Instructor
Blue Ridge Job Corps Center
Marion, Virginia

Maureen Considine, M.A., M.S.

Learning Laboratory Supervisor	ABE/HSE Projects Coordinator
Great Neck Adult Learning Center	National Center for Disability Services
Great Neck, New York	Albertson, New York

Carole Deletiner
Instructor
Hunter College
New York, New York

Patricia Giglio
Remedial Reading Teacher
Johnstown ASACTC
Johnstown, New York

Diane Marinelli Hardison, M.S. Ed.
Mathematics Educator
San Diego, California

Margaret Banker Tinzmann, Ph. D.
Program Associate
The North Central Regional Educational Laboratory
Oak Brook, Illinois

INTRODUCTION

The *Threshold* Pre-GED Programs

Threshold provides a full-range entry-level course for adults whose goal is to earn a high school equivalency diploma. The men and women who use the six *Threshold* programs will learn—and profit from an abundance of sound practice in applying—the writing, problem-solving, and critical-reading and -thinking skills they'll need when they take the GED tests. They will gain a firm grounding in knowledge about social studies and science, and will read many excellent selections from the best of classical and contemporary literature. In short, *Threshold* offers adults the skills, knowledge, and practice that will enable them to approach GED-level test preparation with well-deserved confidence and solid ability.

The *Threshold* Literature Program

The instruction in *Threshold: Cambridge Pre-GED Program in Interpreting Literature and the Arts* is organized by a hierarchy of critical-reading and -thinking skills. Units 1 and 2 cover *comprehension*: Unit 1 concentrates on literal comprehension, and Unit 2 on comprehension that involves making inferences. Unit 3 teaches *application* and *analysis*, the skills that make a reader think critically.

More than 100 selections from literary works by nearly 75 writers provide the vehicles for students to improve and practice their skills. As on the GED, several selections come from works now widely regarded as classics—selections by such writers as Langston Hughes, Flannery O'Connor, and Mark Twain. Also in keeping with the GED, most selections are from contemporary writers of recognized stature: Raymond Carver, Annie Dillard, Andre Dubus, William Least Heat Moon, Toni Morrison, Sam Shepard, Calvin Trillin, and John Updike, to name a few.

All the selections have been painstakingly chosen and carefully positioned in the book. Each meets three important criteria: the readability of each is appropriate for Pre-GED students; each is of high interest to adults; and each, as used, aids the development of critical-reading and -thinking skills. The selections gradually become more challenging as they draw on skills students have sharpened in successive lessons.

The literature program's organization by a hierarchy of skills and its use of fine literary selections similar to those on the GED make *Threshold: Cambridge Pre-GED Program in Interpreting Literature and the Arts* an excellent first course in preparation for the literature test of the GED.

TO THE STUDENT

You will profit in several important ways by using this book as you begin to prepare for the Interpreting Literature and the Arts test of the GED:

- You will improve your reading skills.
- You will expand your knowledge about literature and commentary on the arts.
- You will become acquainted with the writing of several authors.
- You will gain experience in answering questions like those on the GED.
- You will become more confident of your ability.

To Find Out About Your Current Skills in Reading Literature . . .

Take the PRETEST. When you have finished, refer to the ANSWERS AND EXPLANATIONS at the back of this book to check your answers. Then look at the CHARTS that follow the Pretest. They'll give you an idea about which parts of this book you need to concentrate on most.

To Improve Your Reading Skills and Expand Your Knowledge of Literature . . .

Study the LESSONS. They present instruction about reading skills and give examples that show how the various skills can be applied to passages from literature. Some of the examples—called TRY THIS and NOW TRY THIS—let you apply the reading skills. Each lesson ends with an EXERCISE for you to practice your reading skills. The exercises have questions about various types of literature passages.

Read the selections in the INTERPRETING LITERATURE AND THE ARTS READINGS sections, too. They follow the lessons in each unit. The questions in each set of readings give you additional practice with all the reading skills you will have studied up to that point in this book.

To Gain Experience in Answering Questions Like Those on the GED . . .

Take the GED PRACTICE at the end of each unit. The GED Practices are made up of passages and questions like the ones on the literature test of the GED. They offer test-taking experience that you will find useful when you take the GED.

Before you finish with this book, take the POSTTEST. Like the three GED Practices, it is similar to the GED literature test. Look at the CHARTS that follow the Posttest. If you compare your Pretest and Posttest performances, you will probably find that your skills improved as you have worked through this book. The chart can give you an idea about which parts of this book you should review.

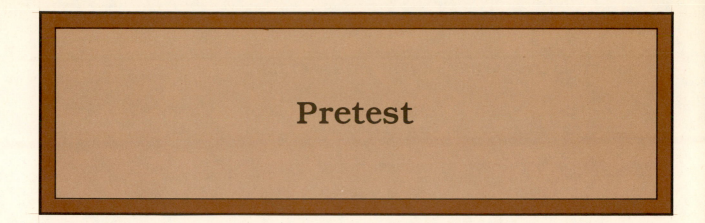

Pretest

The following Pretest is similar to the Interpreting Literature and the Arts Test of the GED. Taking it will help you find out what you need to study most in this book.

The Pretest has 23 multiple-choice items—half as many as there are on the GED. The questions test your understanding of readings from literature and your ability to use and think critically about the information the readings give you.

To begin preparing for the Literature and the Arts Test of the GED, take this Pretest. Work through it at a pace that is comfortable for you. You don't need to study anything before you take the Pretest. The information needed to answer the questions is given in the readings.

The poem "The Bat" in the Pretest says that the bat *loops in crazy figures half the night.*

INTERPRETING LITERATURE AND THE ARTS PRETEST

Directions: Choose the <u>one best answer</u> to each item.

<u>Items 1 to 5</u> refer to the following passage.

WHAT DOES HARRY WANT?

(5)

(10)

(15)

(20)

      Harry had always lived in cities—San Francisco for the last three years, and, before that, Los Angeles, Chicago, and New York. But for a long time he had wanted to move to the country, somewhere in the country. At first he wasn't too clear about where he wanted to go; he just knew he wanted to leave the city to try to start over again. A simpler life was what he had in mind, just the essentials, he said. He was thirty-two years old and was a writer in a way, but he was also an actor and a musician. He played the saxophone, performed occasionally with the Bay City Players, and was writing a first novel. He had been writing the novel since the time he lived in New York. One bleak Sunday afternoon in March, when he had again started talking about a change, a more honest life somewhere in the country, she'd mentioned, jokingly at first, her father's deserted place in the northwestern part of Washington.

      "My God," Harry had said, "you wouldn't mind? Roughing it, I mean? Living in the country like that?"

      "I was born there," she said, laughing. "Remember? I've lived in the country. It's all right. It has advantages. I could live there again. I don't know about you, though, Harry. If it'd be good for you."

      She kept looking at him, serious now. He felt lately that she was always looking at him.

From "How About This?" by Raymond Carver.

1. The main point of the first paragraph is that Harry wants to

   (1) get out of debt
   (2) live close to the land
   (3) escape from his wife
   (4) find a bigger challenge
   (5) live a simpler life

2. Harry seems to be a man who

   (1) is at peace with himself
   (2) feels guilty about something
   (3) is unhappy with his life
   (4) is not very talented
   (5) wants a lot of money and possessions

3. The conversation in the passage took place in

    (1) Chicago
    (2) Los Angeles
    (3) New York
    (4) San Francisco
    (5) Washington

4. The main reason the woman says I don't know about you, though, Harry (Lines 17–18) is probably that Harry

    (1) always lived in cities
    (2) was a writer
    (3) played a saxophone
    (4) was thirty-two years old
    (5) was an actor

5. The tone toward the end of the passage is

    (1) peaceful
    (2) angry
    (3) frightened
    (4) anxious
    (5) amused

Items 6 to 9 refer to the following poem.

WHAT DOES THE POET FIND MOST DISTURBING ABOUT A BAT?

THE BAT

By day the bat is cousin to the mouse.
He likes the attic of an aging house.

His fingers make a house about his head.
His pulse beat is so slow we think him dead.

(5) He loops in crazy figures half the night.
Among the trees that face the corner light.

But when he brushes up against a screen,
We are afraid of what our eyes have seen;

For something is amiss or out of place
(10) When mice with wings can wear a human face.

By Theodore Roethke.

6. According to the author, the bat makes a house

    (1) like a mouse
    (2) with his fingers
    (3) with sticks
    (4) in trees
    (5) like a person

7. According to the poet, the thing that makes a bat a mouse's cousin is that it

   (1) likes old houses
   (2) has fingers
   (3) seems dead
   (4) flies at night
   (5) has wings

8. The poet makes the bat frightening when he says it

   (1) is like a mouse
   (2) likes attics
   (3) has a slow pulse
   (4) flies in crazy figures
   (5) has the face of a human

9. The mood created by the last two stanzas is

   (1) friendly
   (2) calm
   (3) humorous
   (4) disturbing
   (5) playful

Items 10 to 13 are based on the following paragraph.

WHO WILL MAKE A GOOD POET?

W. H. Auden was once asked what advice he would give a young man who wished to become a poet. Auden replied that he would ask the young man why he wanted to write poetry. If the answer was "because I have something important to say," Auden would conclude that there was no hope
(5) for that young man as a poet. If on the other hand the answer was something like "because I like to hang around words and overhear them talking to one another," then that young man was at least interested in a fundamental part of the poetic process and there was hope for him.

From How Does a Poem Mean? by John Ciardi and Miller Williams.

10. When asked what advice he would give to someone who wanted to become a poet, Auden said that he would

    (1) recite a poem for the person
    (2) ask the person a question
    (3) give the person a list of required readings
    (4) discourage the person
    (5) listen to the person's ideas

11. Which of the following best describes the author's purpose in this passage?

    (1) to describe the job of being a poet
    (2) to tell how to write a good poem
    (3) to define what a poem is
    (4) to describe an important characteristic of a poet
    (5) to encourage young people to become poets

12. Auden seems to think that before anything else, a poet must

    (1) appreciate words
    (2) read poetry
    (3) learn to express ideas clearly
    (4) talk to other people
    (5) have important ideas

13. Auden would probably think that a person who has a chance of becoming a poet

    (1) likes to argue political ideas
    (2) hopes to make a lot of money
    (3) feels knowledgeable about human relationships
    (4) enjoys reading a dictionary
    (5) likes to give advice

Items 14 to 18 refer to the following passage from a play.

HAVE JOHN AND TIMMY LEARNED TO RESPECT EACH OTHER MORE?

      JOHN: Can I say something to you?
      TIMMY: Sure.
      JOHN: You won't take it the wrong way?
      TIMMY: No.
(5) JOHN: I owe you an apology.
      TIMMY: For what?
      JOHN: You were always sick; always home from school with one thing or another. I never thought you'd last in the army.
      TIMMY: Neither did I.
(10) JOHN: Really?
      TIMMY: Really.
      JOHN: When Dr. Goldman heard that they took you he said it was ridiculous. When they put you in the infantry he said it was inhuman.
      TIMMY: And when I survived?
(15) JOHN: He said it was a miracle. (They both laugh.) I don't think it was a miracle. I think we just underestimated you . . . Especially me . . . That's what I wanted to apologize for.
      TIMMY: Remember that corny thing you used to recite—about how a boy thinks his father is the greatest guy in the world until he's fifteen. Then the
(20)   doubts start. By the time he's eighteen he's convinced his father is the worst guy in the world. At twenty-five the doubts start again. At thirty it occurs to him that the old man wasn't so bad after all. At forty—
      JOHN: What about it?
      TIMMY: There's some truth to it.

From The Subject Was Roses by Frank Gilroy.

14. You can infer that John and Timmy are

    (1) brothers
    (2) boss and employee
    (3) friends
    (4) neighbors
    (5) father and son

15. In this passage the two characters

    (1) have an argument
    (2) apologize to each other
    (3) complain about the past
    (4) get revenge on each other
    (5) try to hide from the truth

16. Who is He in Line 15?

    (1) John
    (2) Timmy
    (3) the father
    (4) Dr. Goldman
    (5) the greatest guy in the world

17. The stage directions in Line 15 indicate that John and Timmy are feeling

    (1) uncomfortable
    (2) pleasant
    (3) sad
    (4) silly
    (5) foolish

18. If John made a mistake at work, he would probably

    (1) try to hide it
    (2) say it was not a mistake
    (3) blame it on someone else
    (4) accept responsibility for it
    (5) not care about it

Items 19 to 23 refer to the following passage.

WHAT BROUGHT ABOUT THE FALL OF THE PICTURE WEEKLY?

    The most ambitious example of the picture weekly organized according to the principles of the modern business corporation was Life magazine. Life began publishing late in 1936, and was an instant success; by 1940 its circulation had reached three million, and its decline—from a peak
(5) circulation of eight and one-half million copies—did not begin until 1969, by which time television could provide superficial reportage and conventional commentary more quickly than the picture magazines.

From "Photographs in Ink" by John Szarkowski.

19. This passage is mainly about

    (1) the rise and fall of picture weeklies
    (2) principles of modern business corporations
    (3) magazine circulation
    (4) television
    (5) superficial reportage

20. In Line 1 the words <u>picture weekly</u> refer to

    (1) a magazine
    (2) an art show
    (3) a week dedicated to pictures
    (4) a television show
    (5) a commentary on the news

21. The peak circulation of <u>Life</u> magazine was

    (1) about 1 million more than in 1940
    (2) about half the amount it was in 1940
    (3) about the same as in 1940
    (4) twice what it was in 1940
    (5) almost three times what it was in 1940

22. Which of the following is an opinion of the author and not a fact?

    (1) <u>Life</u> began publishing in 1936.
    (2) By 1940, <u>Life</u>'s circulation had reached 3 million.
    (3) <u>Life</u>'s peak circulation was 8 ½ million.
    (4) <u>Life</u>'s circulation began to decline in 1969.
    (5) Television caused <u>Life</u>'s decline in circulation.

23. From this passage, it is possible to conclude that <u>Life</u>

    (1) was once very popular
    (2) has never been very popular
    (3) is popular today
    (4) has always had better news coverage than television
    (5) has always covered the news more quickly than television

Check your answers on page 171.

PRETEST SKILLS CHART

To study the reading skills covered by the items in the Pretest, work through the following parts of this book.

PRETEST CONTENT CHART

The following chart shows the type of reading passage each item in the Pretest refers to.

Type of Literature	Item Number
Nonfiction	10, 11, 12, 13
Fiction	1, 2, 3, 4 ,5
Drama	14, 15, 16, 17, 18
Poetry	6, 7, 8, 9
Commentary	19, 20, 21, 22, 23

UNIT 1

Comprehending What You Read

This unit is about **literal comprehension.** Literal comprehension means understanding what writers tell you directly.

In this unit you will become familiar with some of the types of literature. In Chapter 1 you will find the important details in paragraphs and passages. In Chapter 2 you will identify the topics and main ideas or themes of passages and choose titles for the passages. In Chapter 3 you will practice reading dialogue in fiction, poetry, and drama.

Poet Langston Hughes.
You will read two of his
poems in this unit.

Unit 1 Overview

Chapter 1 Finding Details
Chapter 2 Finding Topics and Main Ideas
Chapter 3 Reading Dialogue

———————————

Interpreting Literature and the Arts **Readings 1**
GED Practice 1

1 FINDING DETAILS

Details are the building blocks of every piece of literature. In the details of any piece of writing you find the answers to who?, what?, where?, when?, and how? Writers tell stories, support arguments, and create moods with details. Sometimes writers are direct. Other times they only give you hints. Both ways of writing depend on details.

Lesson 1

Details in Paragraphs

A paragraph can be as short as one sentence or as long as hundreds of words. The first word of a paragraph is usually indented. That means the first word is set in from the side of the page.

A paragraph is usually a group of sentences about a single topic. Most of the details in a paragraph are about that one topic.

TRY THIS

Complete the following statements. They are based on the first two paragraphs in this lesson.

(1) A paragraph can be as short as just one _____.

(2) A paragraph can go on for _____ of words.

(3) To find the beginning of a paragraph, look for a word that is
_____, or _____.

(4) A paragraph is a group of sentences about _____.

To fill in the blanks, you had to find details. The answers are (1) **sentence**, (2) **hundreds**, (3) **indented**, or **set in from the side of the page**, and (4) **a single topic**.

Spotlight on Types of Literature

In the exercise at the end of this lesson, you will read paragraphs from three different types of literature: a short story, a travel book, and a novel.

Both short stories and novels are **fiction**. Fiction means invented stories. The main difference between short stories and novels is length. A short story may be only one or two pages long. A novel is a book.

Nonfiction is true stories. Books about writers' travels are nonfiction. Biographies—the stories of people's lives—are nonfiction. Diaries and histories are also nonfiction.

TRY THIS

Read the following descriptions of four examples of literature. Then tell whether each is fiction or nonfiction.

Twelve Years by Joel Agee is the true story of an American boy who spent most of his childhood in East Germany. _____

"The Voice" by V.S. Pritchett is a six-page long, imaginary account of a rescue after a bombing in London during World War II. _____

The Mosquito Coast, a novel by Paul Theroux, tells a story about a man who is tired of the modern world. He takes his family to start a new life in a Central American jungle. _____

The Songlines by Bruce Chatwin gives an account of the writer's travels in the sacred land of the native people of Australia. _____

Both *Twelve Years* and *The Songlines* are nonfiction. They are true stories. Since "The Voice" is an *imaginary account*, it is fiction. Since *The Mosquito Coast* is a novel, it is also fiction.

Whenever you read to find specific information, you are reading for details. You probably use this reading skill frequently. For example, you read for details when you use a recipe or a manual that explains how to do something.

When you take the GED, you will read to find details in order to answer questions. In that kind of situation, it's helpful to have the questions in mind as you read. It is also helpful to picture in your mind the people, the things, and the actions you read about.

The next paragraphs are followed by questions about details. Read the questions about each paragraph first. Then, read the paragraph with the questions in mind. Finally, answer the questions.

Questions 1 to 7 refer to the following paragraph. It is the beginning of a short story. As you read it, picture in your mind what the writer describes.

    This old station wagon with Minnesota plates pulls into a parking space in front of the window. There's a man and woman in the front seat, two boys in the back. It's July, temperature's one hundred plus. These people look whipped. There are clothes hanging inside; suitcases, boxes, and such

(5) piled in back. From what Harley and I put together later, that's all they had left after the bank in Minnesota took their house, their pickup, their tractor, the farm implements, and a few cows.

From "The Bridle" by Raymond Carver.

1. Describe the car. _____

2. Who is in the car? _____

3. What month is it? _____

4. What's the temperature? _____

5. What word does the writer use to tell how the people look?
_____

6. What's inside the car with the people? _____

7. Which of the following tells why the car is full of things?
   (1) The family is on vacation, and they need a lot of equipment.
   (2) The family lost the rest of their property to a bank.
   (3) The family has been collecting things on their trip.

Questions 8 to 12 refer to the following paragraph. It is from a book about a writer's experiences on a trip around the United States. He avoided wide interstate highways and drove only on smaller roads, which were colored blue on his map. He got the title for his book from the blue lines on the map. The paragraph is about a Hopi Indian reservation in Arizona. Think about the conditions on the reservation.

Hopi Indians in sunrise flute ceremony at Oraibi in Arizona.

I couldn't see how anyone could survive a year in this severe land, yet Hopis, like other desert life, are patient and clever and not at all desperate; they have lasted here for ten centuries by using tiny terraced plots that catch spring rain and produce a desert-hardy species of blue corn, as well (5) as squash, onions, beans, peppers, melons, apricots, peaches. The bristlecone pine of American Indians, Hopis live where almost nothing else will, thriving long in adverse conditions: poor soil, drought, temperature extremes, high winds. Those give life to the bristlecone and the Hopi.

From *Blue Highways* by William Least Heat Moon.

8. The writer says that the Hopis are _____ and _____ and not at all _____.

9. For how long have the Hopis been on their land?

_____

10. What eight crops do the Hopis grow? _____ , _____ , _____ , _____ , _____ , _____ , _____ , and _____

11. The writer compares the Hopis to which of the following plants?

    (1) the bristlecone pine

    (2) the peach tree

    (3) the pepper plant

12. Name the four conditions that the Hopis live with. _____ , _____ , _____ , and _____

Questions 13 to 19 refer to the following paragraph. It is a long paragraph from a novel. This paragraph is about the hero of the book, a young man nicknamed Milkman. Lena is his sister. Think about the way Milkman deals with his discovery.

        By the time Milkman was fourteen he had noticed that one of his legs was shorter than the other. When he stood barefoot and straight as a pole, his left foot was about half an inch off the floor. So he never stood straight; he slouched or leaned or stood with a hip thrown out

(5) and he never told anybody about it— ever. When Lena said, "Mama, what is he walking like *that* for?" he said, "I'll walk any way I want to, including over your ugly face." Ruth said, "Be quiet, you two. It's just growing pains, Lena." Milkman knew better. It wasn't a limp—not at all—just the suggestion of one, but it looked like an affected walk, the

(10) strut of a very young man trying to appear more sophisticated than he was. It bothered him and he acquired movements and habits to disguise what to him was a burning defect. He sat with his left ankle on his right knee, never the other way around. And he danced each new dance with a curious stiff-legged step that the girls loved and other boys

(15) eventually copied. The deformity was mostly in his mind. Mostly, but not completely, for he did have shooting pains in that leg after several hours on a basketball court. He favored it, believed it was polio, and felt secretly connected to the late President Roosevelt for that reason. Even when everybody was raving about Truman because he had set up a

(20) Committee on Civil Rights, Milkman secretly preferred FDR and felt very close to him. Closer in fact, to him than to his own father, for Macon had no imperfection and age seemed to strengthen him. Milkman feared his father, respected him, but knew, because of the leg, that he could never emulate him. So he differed from him as much as he

(25) dared. Macon was clean-shaven; Milkman was desperate for a mustache. Macon wore bow ties; Milkman wore four-in-hands. Macon didn't part his hair; Milkman had a part shaved into his. Macon hated tobacco; Milkman tried to put a cigarette in his mouth every fifteen minutes. Macon hoarded his money; Milkman gave his away. But he

(30) couldn't help sharing with Macon his love of good shoes and fine thin

socks. And he did try, as his father's employee, to do the work the way Macon wanted it done.

From *The Song of Solomon* by Toni Morrison.

13. What does Milkman discover in the first sentence?

_____

14. True or false? Milkman liked to talk about his problem. _____

15. When did Milkman's problem cause him real pain?

_____

16. Which president did Milkman feel connected to? _____

17. Who is Macon? _____

18. Which of the following does NOT describe one of the differences between Macon and Milkman?

   (1) Macon shaved; Milkman wanted a mustache.
   (2) Macon never smoked; Milkman smoked a lot.
   (3) Macon saved money; Milkman gave his money away.
   (4) Macon liked good shoes; Milkman hated them.

19. According to the last sentence, Milkman tried to do what his father wanted

   (1) on the basketball court
   (2) at work
   (3) in school

Check your answers on page 172.

Lesson 2

Details in Passages

A **passage** is any part of a longer piece of writing. A passage itself may seem quite long. In Exercise 1 on page 12 you read passages of only one paragraph. On the GED most of the passages are longer than one paragraph.

As with paragraphs, most of the details in a passage are about its topic. The details help to make the topic clear.

When you read a passage, notice who the **narrator** is. The narrator is the person who tells the story. The narrator may be a character invented by the author. Writers of fiction often use one of

Spotlight On Poem Titles

Some reading passages on the GED are poems. When you read a poem, pay attention to its title. The title often gives a clue to the main topic or theme of the poem. The title may also help you understand why the poet has chosen certain details.

their characters to tell the details of a story. The narrator may be the author himself (or herself).

As you read a passage, you get details through the narrator's eyes. Try to imagine what the narrator is thinking. Try to guess what the narrator is about to tell you.

TRY THIS

Answer the questions about the following poem by Robert Frost—a poet who worked as a farmer, a mill laborer, a shoemaker, and a school teacher.

As you read this poem, think about the narrator. Try to figure out what the narrator is doing and why he puts down the tool he is using.

Note: Some of the passages in this book include words you may not know. Brief definitions of such words appear throughout the book. Two words from the following poem are defined for you.

A TIME TO TALK

When a friend calls to me from the road
And slows his horse to a **meaning** walk,
I don't stand still and look around
On all the hills I haven't hoed,
(5)   And shout from where I am, "What is it?"
No, not as there is a time to talk.
I thrust my hoe in the mellow ground,
Blade-end up and five feet tall,
And **plod:** I go up to the stone wall
(10)   For a friendly visit.

From *A Pocket Book of Robert Frost's Poems.*

> *Meaning:* with purpose
> *Plod:* walk slowly

What kind of event does the narrator mention in the first line of the poem? _____

What tool does the narrator mention in Line 7? _____

Which of the following tells what the narrator does when a friend comes to visit while he is working?

(1) He tells his friend that he's sorry but he has to get his work done.

(2) He tells his friend to help him with his work.

(3) He stops work to visit with his friend.

In the first line the narrator mentions times when a friend calls him from the road. The narrator mentions a hoe. Choice (3) is the correct answer to the last question. Notice that the title, "A Time to Talk," suggests what the narrator would do if a friend came to visit.

As you read in Lesson 1, keep in mind that it is often best to read the questions first and then to read the passage. This is a good way to prepare yourself to find the details needed to answer the questions.

EXERCISE 2

Read the following passages and answer the questions about them.

Questions 1 to 6 refer to the following passage from a book by the writer and television personality Studs Terkel. The passage is from an interview with Leonel I. Castillo, the former director of the United States Immigration and Naturalization Service. In the interview he describes a typical young immigrant worker.

He's the bright kid in the family. The slow one might not make it, might get killed. The one who's sickly can't make the trip. He couldn't walk through the desert. He's not gonna be too old, too young, too destitute, or too slow. He's the brightest and the best.

(5) He's gonna be the first hook, the first pioneer coming into an alien society, the United States. He might be here in Chicago. He works as a busboy all night long. They pay him minimum or less, and work him hard. He'll never complain. He might even thank his boss. He'll say as little as possible because he doesn't want anyone to know what his

(10) status is. He will often live in his apartment, except for the time he goes to work or to church or to a dance. He will stay in and watch TV. If he makes a hundred a week, he will manage to send back twenty- five. All

over the country, if you go to a Western Union office on the weekend, you'll find a lot of people there sending money orders. In a southwest (15) office, like Dallas, Western Union will tell you seventy-five percent of their business is money orders to Mexico.

After the kid learns a bit, because he's healthy and young and energetic, he'll probably get another job as a busboy. He'll work at another place as soon as the shift is over. He'll try to work his way up (20) to be a waiter. He'll work incredible hours. He doesn't care about union scale, he doesn't care about conditions, about humiliations. He accepts all this as his fate.

From *American Dreams: Lost and Found* by Studs Terkel.

1. In what city does the interview take place? _____

2. What is the first job of the young worker described in the passage? _____

3. According to the passage, each of the following is **true** of the typical immigrant worker EXCEPT:
   (1) He saves all his money for himself.
   (2) He leaves his apartment only to go to work, to church, or to a dance.
   (3) He stays in and watches TV.

4. According to the author, many people go to **Western Union** offices on weekends to
   (1) wait for money from home
   (2) pick up telegrams
   (3) send money orders

5. True or false? The young immigrant worker worries about not getting union pay. _____

6. The narrator thinks that a typical young immigrant worker
   (1) demands a lot and expects to be treated like other Americans
   (2) is disappointed with the United States and hopes to get back to his country soon
   (3) is willing to work long hours and doesn't care about working conditions

Questions 7 to 12 refer to the following passage—another from the book *Blue Highways*. This passage is about a village on the Hopi reservation.

Clinging to the southern tip of Third **Mesa** was ancient Oraibi, most probably the oldest continuously occupied village in the United States.

Somehow the stone and adobe have been able to hang on to the **precipitous** edge since the twelfth century. More than eight hundred Hopis lived at (5) Oraibi in 1901—now only a few. All across the reservation I'd seen no more than a dozen people, and on the dusty streets of the old town I saw just one bent woman struggling against the wind. But somewhere there must have been more.

To this strangest of American villages the Franciscan father, Tomas (10) Garces, came in 1776 from Tucson with gifts and "true religion." Hopis permitted him to stay at Oraibi, looking then as now if you excluded an occasional television antenna, but they refused his gifts and god, and, on the fourth day of July, sent him off disheartened.

From *Blue Highways* by William Least Heat Moon.

Mesa: high, flat land

Indian stone-and-adobe village atop a mesa in Arizona.

7. What is the name of the village? _____

8. What was the population of the village in 1901? _____

9. The one person the writer saw on the streets of the old town was

   (1) a worker hanging on to the edge of a cliff
   (2) a bent woman
   (3) a Franciscan father

10. Who was Tomas Garces? _____

11. The writer says that in 1776 the village looked as it does now except for what detail?

   (1) stone and adobe buildings
   (2) dusty streets
   (3) television antennas

12. Which of the following tells how the Hopis treated Father Tomas Garces?

   (1) They accepted him but not his beliefs.
   (2) They tortured him and drove him away.
   (3) They invited him to join their tribe.

Questions 13 to 18 refer to the following poem. It is a translation of an old Chinese poem. The poet, Chu Hsi, lived from 1130 to 1200. Think about the poet's wish.

THE FARM BY THE LAKE

For ten miles the mountains rise
Above the lake. The beauty
Of water and mountain is
Impossible to describe.
(5) In the glow of evening
A traveller sits in front
Of an inn, sipping wine.
The moon shines above a
Little bridge and a single
(10) Fisherman. Around the farm
A bamboo fence descends to
The water. I chat with an
Old man about work and crops.
Maybe, when the years have come
(15) When I can lay aside my
Cap and robe of office,
I can take a little boat
And come back to this place.

From *One Hundred Poems from the Chinese* by Kenneth Rexroth.

13. What does the poet say about the beauty of water and mountain? _____

14. What is the traveller mentioned in Line 6 doing? _____

15. Who does the narrator talk to? _____

16. What do they talk about? _____

17. When he talks about laying *aside* his *cap and robe of office* (Lines 15–16), the narrator is probably referring to

    (1) the responsibilities of his job
    (2) his winter clothes
    (3) his luggage

18. The narrator suggests that he

    (1) is bored and wants to go home
    (2) plans to stay where he is
    (3) hopes to return to the place someday.

Check your answers on page 173.

2 FINDING TOPICS AND MAIN IDEAS

In Chapter 1, you practiced finding details in passages. In this chapter you will see how writers use details to focus a reader's attention on a topic. You will also see how writers sometimes use details to make a special point or state a main idea about a topic.

Lesson 3

Topics

The details in a paragraph or passage are usually **about a single topic**. The details offer clues about what the topic is.

Pay close attention to the first sentence in a paragraph. It may tell you the topic of what is to follow.

TRY THIS

Read the following paragraph from a short story and answer the question that follows it.

> It's so hard to be nice to people. It's something you have to learn. I try to be nice, but it's complicated. You start feeling guilty for your own failures of generosity at just about the same point in life when you start feeling angry, even less willing to give. The two
> (5) feelings collide—feeling gracious and feeling mean.
>
> From "With Jazz" by Bobbie Ann Mason.

The topic of the paragraph is
   (1) generosity and anger
   (2) being nice to people
   (3) feeling guilty about failures

Both Choices (1) and (3) are mentioned in the paragraph, but Choice (2) is the topic. The first sentence of the paragraph states the topic. The sentences that follow tell why it's hard to be nice. The author says that you have to learn to be nice, that it's complicated to be nice, that you feel guilty when generosity fails you, and that you start feeling anger.

The first sentence does not always tell the topic of a paragraph. Sometimes no single sentence tells the topic. However, repeated words or phrases are clues that can help you identify the topic.

NOW TRY THIS

Read the next paragraph. Watch for repeated words that suggest the topic.

It was a fine May morning when we set out, Mrs. Rundlett and I and a friend of mine, to take a look at five houses. I do not have happy memories of that day; I was too anxious, and much of the time too depressed. The fact is that a house for sale has a slightly **sinister**
(5) atmosphere; life has gone stale in its abandoned shell. It happened that those we saw were far from each other, so that we **trundled** through unknown country for what seemed like hours, and I was over-aware of scrubby woods and sad stone walls with their silent testament to the fact that all this land had been cleared a hundred
(10) years or more ago and then grown back to jungle. One of the houses, it is true, was beautiful and stood in an open sunny meadow, but it was huge, still furnished, and smelled of other people's lives. Why had they left, I wondered? I had never hunted a house before and was unprepared for the shock of this public invasion of private
(15) atmospheres. By eleven o'clock I was almost ready to call off the whole thing, except that it did seem foolish not to take a look at the last house on the list, that **dilapidated** eighteenth-century farmhouse in the village of Nelson.

From *Plant Dreaming Deep* by May Sarton.

sinister: threatening, evil
trundled: rolled, wheeled, drove
dilapidated: run down, worn

The topic of the paragraph is
  (1) a morning in May
  (2) a trip through the countryside
  (3) shopping for a house

The writer mentions *a fine May morning* in the first sentence. She also mentions things found in the countryside, such as *scrubby woods* and *sad stone walls,* but neither Choice (1) nor Choice (2) is the topic. Look at the following phrases from the paragraph. The word *house* or *houses* is repeated in each: *take a look at five houses, a house for sale, one of the houses, never hunted a house before,* and *the last house.* The repeated words suggest the topic. Choice (3) is correct.

Choosing A Title

A good way to identify the topic of a passage is to give the passage a title. A title is a kind of summary of the ideas in a passage. Paying attention to the details in a passage can help you decide what its title could be.

TRY THIS

Read the next passage and answer the questions that follow it. The passage is from an interview with Vernon Jarrett, a popular writer for a Chicago newspaper. He talks about his parents' generation in the South. Many of the people he remembers were the children of slaves. The questions are about details in the passage that can help you choose a title for the passage.

> Some Sundays in church when they started singin' those old hymns, those people would start laughing and answering each other from across the room. We kids couldn't understand what on earth they were laughing about. I remember one of us got up enough guts
> (5) to ask what was so funny. They'd say: "We're not really laughin', you youngsters would never understand it." They were really laughing about the fact that they had survived: Here we are sitting up here, free. There are our kids here with us. I've got a home, and my daughter is a schoolteacher. That's what I used to hear my
> (10) grandmother say.
> The thing I remember about these folks was the immense dignity and pride in the way they walked. They walked like straight sticks. They made us stand like that. This always slays me, that all of us had to stand erect. They would go around asking you: "Boy, aren't you
> (15) gonna be somebody when you grow up?" They'd always say: "I'm never gonna live to see it."

From *American Dreams: Lost and Found* by Studs Terkel.

Mr. Jarrett says that the older people were laughing about the fact that they had _____.

Mr. Jarrett's grandmother expressed pride in four things. What were they? _____, _____, _____, and _____

What does Mr. Jarrett say that he remembers most about the older people?
 (1) their singing
 (2) their laughing
 (3) their dignity and pride

Which of the following titles best fits this passage?
 (1) The Pleasures of Church Music
 (2) The Generation Gap
 (3) The Pride of a Generation of People

The older people were laughing about the fact that they had survived.

Mr. Jarrett's grandmother was proud that the people were free, that their children were with them, that she had a house, and that her daughter was a schoolteacher.

Mr. Jarrett remembers most (3) their dignity and pride.

Because the writer talks about the older people's happiness in their survival, their pride, and their dignity, Choice (3) is the best title in the list.

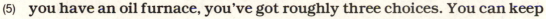

EXERCISE 3

Read the next three passages and answer the questions about them. Most of the questions are about details that will help you recognize the topic or choose a title.

Questions 1 to 4 refer to the following paragraph. It is from an article about the state of Vermont.

It's a rare Vermont winter that doesn't have one stretch of weather when it's twenty below every night, and not much above zero even at midday. Keeping warm during such a spell is either difficult or expensive —sometimes both. If you're living in a big old house in the country, and if (5) you have an oil furnace, you've got roughly three choices. You can keep

the thermostat up at 70 and go broke. You can turn it down to 55, put your family in long underwear, and shiver. Or you can heat two or three rooms with wood stoves, and move in, relying on the furnace only to keep the pipes in the rest of the house from freezing. That's what most of us do.

From "A Cool Morning in Vermont" by Noel Perrin.

1. The words *a spell* in Line 3 probably refer to

    (1) a place
    (2) a time during the day
    (3) the weather

2. The writer says that if you keep the thermostat at 70, you may

    (1) go broke
    (2) still be cold
    (3) heat only two or three rooms

3. According to the author, most people handle the cold weather in Vermont by

    (1) turning the thermostat up to 70
    (2) wearing long underwear
    (3) heating part of the house with wood stoves

4. The topic of the paragraph is

    (1) the advantages of a wood stove
    (2) keeping warm during a Vermont winter
    (3) the importance of wool clothes

Questions 5 to 9 refer to the following passage from a book about food.

People ask me: Why do you write about food, and eating and drinking? Why don't you write about the struggle for power and security, and about love, the way others do?

They ask it accusingly, as if I were somehow gross, unfaithful to
(5) the honor of my craft.

The easiest answer is to say that, like most other humans, I am hungry. But there is more than that. It seems to me that our three basic needs, for food and security and love, are so mixed and mingled and entwined that we cannot straightly think of one without the others. So
(10) it happens that when I write of hunger, I am really writing about love and the hunger for it, and warmth and the love of it and the hunger for it . . . and then the warmth and richness and fine reality of hunger satisfied . . . and it is all one.

I tell about myself, and how I ate bread on a lasting hillside, or
(15) drank red wine in a room now blown to bits, and it happens without my

willing it that I am telling too about the people with me then, and their other deeper needs for love and happiness.

There is food in the bowl, and more often than not, because of what honesty I have, there is nourishment in the heart, to feed the wilder,
(20) more insistent hungers. We must eat. If, in the face of that dread fact, we can find other nourishment, and tolerance and compassion for it, we'll be no less full of human dignity.

There is a communion of more than our bodies when bread is broken and wine drunk. And that is my answer, when people ask me:
(25) Why do you write about hunger, and not wars or love?

From *The Gastronomical Me* by M. F. K. Fisher.

5. What three topics do people suggest the writer should write about? _____, _____, _____

6. What does the writer mean by her *craft* in Line 5?

   (1) cooking
   (2) writing
   (3) wine producing

7. What does the writer call our three basic needs? _____, _____, _____

8. Which of the following would the writer probably NOT agree with?

   (1) The need for food is mixed with other human needs.
   (2) Food is the only topic that interests the writer.
   (3) When the writer writes about food, she also writes about the people she shared it with.

9. Which of the following titles best fits this passage?

   (1) Why I Write about Food
   (2) Why I Like to Cook
   (3) How I Got Started as a Writer

Questions 10 to 15 refer to the following passage. In it a writer describes something that happened during a trip to Mexico.

In my good moments, I've been able to say what I needed to say in Spanish, although not in a way that was likely to attract compliments on my grammar and syntax. In my bad moments, my attempts to speak Spanish have a lot in common with my attempts to speak Italian, which
(5) is to say that they lean heavily on gestures. I have always had trouble understanding Spanish; there have been times when a paragraph of Spanish has sounded to me like one long word.

Even when I seem to be doing pretty well in Spanish, I can run out

(10) of it, the way someone might run out of flour or eggs. A few years after I passed up the chance to stay in Madrid, some friends and I went to Baja California to mark an occasion I can no longer remember, and I became the group's spokesman to the owner of our motel, a Mrs. Gonzales, who spoke no English. Toward the end of a very long evening, as I listened to her complain about some excess of celebration on our part, I

(15) suddenly realized that I had run out of Spanish. It wasn't merely that I couldn't think of the Spanish words for what I wanted to say ("I am **mortified**, Mrs. Gonzales, to learn that someone in our group might have behaved in a manner so inappropriate, not to say disgusting"). I couldn't think of any Spanish words at all. Desperately rummaging

(20) around in the small bin of Spanish in my mind, I could come up with nothing but the title of a Calderon play I had once read, to no lasting effect, in a Spanish literature course.

"Mrs. Gonzales," I said. "Life is a dream."

She looked impressed and, I must say, surprised. She told me that I

(25) had said something really quite profound. I shrugged. It seemed the appropriately modest response; even if it hadn't been, it would have been all I could do until I managed to borrow a cup of Spanish from a neighbor. Eventually I came to look back on the experience as just about the only time I was truly impressive in a foreign language.

From "*Abigail y Yo*" by Calvin Trillin.

---

mortified: ashamed

---

10. How does the writer describe his Spanish in his good moments?

    (1) He can say what he needs to.
    (2) He mixes Italian with his Spanish.
    (3) He depends on gestures.

11. Who is Mrs. Gonzales? _____

12. What did Mrs. Gonzales complain about?

    (1) the celebrations of the writer and his friends
    (2) the writer's bad Spanish
    (3) the writer's failure to pay his bill

13. What the author says to Mrs. Gonzales was, in fact,

    (1) an insult
    (2) a joke in Italian
    (3) the title of a play

14. Which word does NOT describe Mrs. Gonzales' reaction to what the writer said in Spanish?

   (1) impressed
   (2) surprised
   (3) amused

15. Which of the following phrases from the passage would work best as a title for the passage?

   (1) Trouble Understanding Spanish
   (2) The Appropriately Modest Response
   (3) The Only Time I Was Truly Impressive in a Foreign Language

Check your answers on page 173.

Lesson 4

Main Ideas

Usually a writer makes a special point about the topic of a paragraph or a passage. In a paragraph and in most nonfiction, this point is called the **main idea.** In most passages of fiction and in poetry, the special point the writer makes is called the **theme.**

   To identify a main idea or a theme, first find the topic of a passage. Then think about the details the writer provides. Think about the arguments he or she makes and the ideas that are emphasized. Finally, consider the details, the arguments, and the important points all together. Decide what special point they make about the topic.

Spotlight on Commentary

Commentary on the arts is writing about the visual arts, such as painting and sculpture, or about the performing arts, such as music, film, dance, and theater. Commentary can be as brief as a review in a newspaper or as long as a book.

TRY THIS

Read the following paragraph from a book of commentary. Find the topic and notice what the writer says about it. Then answer the questions that follow the paragraph.

All books on understanding music are agreed about one point: You can't develop a better appreciation of the art merely by reading a book about it. If you want to understand music better, you can do nothing more important than listen to it. Nothing can possibly take (5) the place of listening to music. Everything that I have to say in this book is said about an experience that you can only get outside this book. Therefore, you will probably be wasting your time in reading it unless you make a firm resolve to hear a great deal more music than you have in the past. All of us, professionals and nonprofessionals, (10) are forever trying to deepen our understanding of the art. Reading a book may sometimes help us. But nothing can replace the prime consideration—listening to music itself.

From *What to Listen for in Music* by Aaron Copland.

The words *the art* used in both Lines 2 and 11 refer to
(1) painting
(2) literature
(3) music
(4) sculpture

Which of the following is the topic of the paragraph?
(1) reading
(2) music
(3) experience
(4) understanding

Below are three sentences from the paragraph. Which of them comes closest to telling the main idea the writer makes about the topic?

(1) If you want to understand music better, you can do nothing more important than listen to it.
(2) All of us, professionals and nonprofessionals, are forever trying to deepen our understanding of the art.
(3) Reading a book may sometimes help us.

The only art the writer mentions is music, Choice (3).

The topic of the paragraph is music, Choice (2). The writer uses the word *music* five times.

The main idea of the paragraph is Choice (1). Choice (2) is an observation about many people. Like Choice (3), it is not the main idea, but it supports the main idea. The author emphasizes the main idea by repeating it. He says, *Nothing can possibly take the place of listening to music* (Lines 4–5). Again in the last sentence he says, *But nothing can replace the prime consideration—listening to music itself.*

Spotlight on Essays

An essay is a short—not as long as a book—piece of writing about personal reactions to something.

NOW TRY THIS

The next paragraph is from an essay. Read the paragraph and answer the questions that follow.

> Appealing work places are to be avoided. One wants a room with no view, so imagination can dance with memory in the dark. When I furnished this study seven years ago, I pushed the long desk against a blank wall, so I could not see from either window. Once,
> (5) fifteen years ago, I wrote in a cinder-block cell over a parking lot. It overlooked a tar-and-gravel roof. This pine shed under trees is not quite so good as the cinder-block study was, but it will do.

From "Schedules" by Annie Dillard.

The writer mentions a cinder-block cell and a pine shed. According to the paragraph, these are places where the writer has
(1) slept
(2) cooked
(3) worked

Which of the following is the topic of the paragraph?
(1) rooms
(2) work places
(3) sheds

The author states the main idea of the paragraph by saying that
(1) appealing work places are to be avoided
(2) imagination can dance with memory in the dark
(3) this pine shed will do

The cinder-block cell and the pine shed are places where the writer has worked, Choice (3).

The topic of the paragraph is work places, Choice (2). Notice that the topic of the first sentence is also work places.

The main idea of the paragraph is stated in Choice (1). The author believes that a simple work place, like a pine shed or a cinder-block cell, allows the imagination to *dance with memory in the dark*. She pushed the desk in her current work place against a blank wall. She used to work in a cell with a view of only a tar-and-gravel roof.

Read the following passages and answer the questions about them. Some of the questions are about the details that can help you find the main idea.

Questions 1 to 4 refer to the following paragraph. It is from a short story. Think about the narrator's worries.

This blind man, an old friend of my wife's, he was on his way to spend the night. His wife had died. So he was visiting the dead wife's relatives in Connecticut. He called my wife from his in-laws'. Arrangements were made. He would come by train, a five-hour trip, and
(5) my wife would meet him at the station. She hadn't seen him since she worked for him one summer in Seattle ten years ago. But she and the blind man had kept in touch. They made tapes and mailed them back and forth. I wasn't enthusiastic about his visit. He was no one I knew. And his being blind bothered me. My idea of blindness came from the
(10) movies. In the movies, the blind moved slowly and never laughed. Sometimes they were led by seeing-eye dogs. A blind man in my house was not something I looked forward to.

From "Cathedral" by Raymond Carver.

1. Who is the blind man in the story?

   (1) a friend of the narrator
   (2) an in-law
   (3) a friend of the narrator's wife

2. True or false? The narrator is happy that the blind man is coming to visit. _____

3. Where does the narrator say he got his idea about blindness?

   _____

4. Below are four sentences from the paragraph. Which one tells the theme or main idea best?

   (1) This blind man, an old friend of my wife's, he was on his way to spend the night.
   (2) And his being blind bothered me.
   (3) He was no one I knew.
   (4) A blind man in my house was not something I looked forward to.

Questions 5 to 8 refer to the following poem from the collection *Spoon River Anthology.* Each poem is named for a person who lived in the imaginary town Spoon River. Each poem is an epitaph for the character named in the title. (An epitaph is a brief statement that recalls a person who has died.) In these poems, each person tells his own epitaph.

ABEL MELVENY

I bought every kind of machine that's known—
Grinders, shellers, planters, mowers,
Mills and rakes and ploughs and threshers—
And all of them stood in the rain and sun,
(5) Getting rusted, warped and battered,
For I had no sheds to store them in,
And no use for most of them.
And toward the last, when I thought it over,
There by my window, growing clearer
(10) About myself, as my pulse slowed down,
And I looked at one of the mills I bought—
Which I didn't have the slightest need of,
As things turned out, and I never ran—
A fine machine, once brightly varnished,
(15) And eager to do its work,
Now with its paint washed off—
I saw myself as a good machine
That Life had never used.

From *Spoon River Anthology* by Edgar Lee Masters.

5. *Grinders, shellers, planters,* and *mowers* (Line 2) are examples of machines that Abel Melveny

   (1) used in his work
   (2) sold in his store
   (3) repaired in his shop
   (4) bought and never used

6. Abel Melveny compares himself to

   (1) a farmer
   (2) a mechanic
   (3) a machine

7. The words *And toward the last* in Line 8 refer to

   (1) the time shortly before Abel Melveny died
   (2) the machine he had just bought
   (3) the view from his window

8. In which of the following pairs of lines is the main idea, or theme, stated?

   (1) Lines 6–7
   (2) Lines 9–10
   (3) Lines 17–18

Questions 9 to 14 refer to the following passage. It is the beginning of another short story by Raymond Carver. Think about the main character's problems and the way he thinks he can solve them.

As Al saw it, there was only one solution. He had to get rid of the dog without Betty or the kids finding out about it. At night. It would have to be done at night. He would simply drive Suzy—well, someplace, later he'd decide where—open the door, push her out, drive away. The
(5) sooner the better. He felt relieved making the decision. Any action was better than no action at all, he was becoming convinced.

It was Sunday. He got up from the kitchen table where he had been eating a late breakfast by himself and stood by the sink, hands in his pockets. Nothing was going right lately. He had enough to contend with
(10) without having to worry about a stinking dog. They were laying off at Aerojet when they should be hiring. The middle of the summer, defense contracts let all over the country and Aerojet was talking of cutting back. *Was* cutting back, in fact, a little more every day. He was no safer than anyone else even though he'd been there two years going on three.
(15) He got along with the right people, all right, but seniority or friendship, either one, didn't mean a damn these days. If your number was up, that

was that—and there was nothing anybody could do. They got ready to lay off, they laid off. Fifty, a hundred men at a time.

From "Jerry and Molly and Sam" by Raymond Carver.

9. Near the beginning of the passage, Al decides to

   (1) get a new job
   (2) get rid of the dog
   (3) get away from his wife and children

10. When does Al plan to act on his decision?

    (1) after he has discussed his plans with his wife and kids
    (2) after a night's sleep
    (3) as soon as possible

11. Why does Al feel relieved in Line 5?

    (1) He has finally made a decision.
    (2) He knows his job is secure.
    (3) Sunday was the one day he could relax.

12. What was happening at Aerojet?

    (1) Al was getting a raise.
    (2) Workers were being laid off.
    (3) Business was improving.

13. True or false? Al knew that his ability to get along with people would save his job. _____

14. Which of the following sentences best tells the theme, or main idea, of the passage?

    (1) Any action was better than no action at all, he was becoming convinced.
    (2) Nothing was going right lately.
    (3) He was no safer than anyone else even though he'd been there two years going on three.

Check your answers on page 174.

Chapter

3 READING DIALOGUE

Dialogue is conversation between two or more people. Novels and short stories often contain dialogues among the characters. Dialogue forms the main part of most plays. Some poems also contain dialogues.

In this chapter you will practice reading dialogue from short stories, novels, a travel book, plays, and a poem.

Lesson 5

Dialogue in Fiction and Poetry

In life, we learn a lot about a person from what he or she says. In literature, writers often use the exact words of a character to reveal the character's nature.

Writers usually use quotation marks (" ") around the exact words the characters say. They also use a new paragraph each time a different character speaks.

Compare the following two short passages.

A: When the clouds got darker, John said, "Fred, I think we're lost." "Trust me," Fred replied. "I'm sure we can find the path."

B: When the clouds got darker, John told Fred that he thought they were lost. Fred told John to trust him because he was sure they could find the path.

In Passage A, you read the exact words of John and Fred. Their words are inside the quotation marks. In Passage B, you read *about* their dialogue.

Notice that John, in Passage A, speaks in the first paragraph. When Fred speaks, a new paragraph begins.

TRY THIS

Read the next passage and answer the questions that follow it. Pay close attention to who says each line of dialogue. Each paragraph indentation means a change in speakers.

Ellen looked upset. She said, ''What have you done now, Bill?''

''I haven't done anything,'' Bill answered.

''Then why is Sam mad again? He just called, and he sounded furious.''

''You know Sam. He's always mad about something.''

''Yes, and I know you, too.''

Name the three characters mentioned in this passage.

_____, _____, and _____

The dialogue takes place between what two characters?

_____ and _____

Who says, *Then why is Sam mad again? He just called, and he sounded furious?* _____

Who says, *You know Sam. He's always mad about something?*

_____

The three characters in the passage are Ellen, Bill, and Sam.

The dialogue takes place between Ellen and Bill.

Ellen says, *Then why is Sam mad again? He just called, and he sounded furious.*

Bill says, *You know Sam. He's always mad about something.*

EXERCISE 5

Read each passage and answer the questions about them.

Questions 1 to 7 refer to the following passage from *Blue Highways.* The passage contains a dialogue between the author and a man restoring an old house in a small town in Kentucky.

At the west end of Main, a man stripping siding from a small, two-story house had exposed a log cabin. I stopped to watch him straighten the doorway. To get a better perspective, he came to the sidewalk, eyed the lintel, then looked at me. ''It's tilting, isn't it?'' he
(5)   said.

''There's a little list to it, but you could live with that.''

''I want it right.'' He went to the door, set up a jack, measured, then leaned into it. The timbers creaked and squared up. He shoved a couple of two-by-fours behind the lintel to hold it true then cranked down the
(10)   jack. ''Come in for a look,'' he said. ''After a hundred and fifty years, she's not likely to fall down today.''

A renovated two-story house made of logs *bigger than railway ties . . . locked in dovetails.*

"That's before people started jacking around with it."

The interior, bare of plaster and lath, leaked a deep smell of old timbers. Bigger than railway ties, the logs lay locked in dovetails, all (15) careful work done only with ax, adz, froe, and wedge. The man, Bob Andriot, asked what I thought. "It's a beauty. How long have you been at it?"

"Ten days. We want to move in the first of April."

"You're going to live here?"

(20) "My wife and I have a picture-framing and interior design shop. We're moving it out of our house. We just bought this place."

"Did you know the log cabin was underneath the siding?"

"We thought it possible. Shape of the house and the low windows looked right. We knew some were along Main." He went to the door. (25) "That little house across the street. Could be one under the siding. A lot of cabins still buried under asphalt shingles, and nobody knows it. I've heard Kentucky's got more log houses than any other state."

From *Blue Highways* by William Least Heat Moon.

1. A *lintel* (Line 4) is probably a part of a

   (1) tool box
   (2) street sign
   (3) doorway

2. In Line 4, who says, *It's tilting, isn't it?*—the author or the man working on the house? _____

3. What are the *ax, adz, froe, and wedge* in Line 15?

    (1) names of log-cabin builders

    (2) kinds of logs

    (3) kinds of tools

4. What is the name of the man working on the house? _____

5. How long has the man been working on the house? _____

6. In Line 19, who asks, *You're going to live here?*—the author or the man working on the house? _____

7. What two clues suggested that the house was a log cabin under its siding? _____ and _____

Questions 8 to 13 refer to the following passage from a novel. The dialogue takes place between a man named Sydney and his wife Ondine. They live on a Caribbean island in the house of a rich, retired man. Sydney, his wife, and their boss have moved to the island from Philadelphia.

In this passage the author never uses Ondine's name, and she uses Sydney's name only twice. You must read carefully to understand who is saying each line. Remember that each new paragraph indicates a shift in speakers. In this passage the dialogue shifts back and forth between Sydney and his wife, Ondine.

What the devil does he do in there, she had asked him.

"Relaxes a little, that's all. Drinks a bit, reads, listens to his records."

"Can't nobody spend every day in a shed for three years without being up to some devilment," she said.

(5) "It's not a shed," said Sydney. "It's a greenhouse I keep telling you."

"Whatever you call it."

"He grows hydrangeas in there. And dahlias."

"If he wants hydrangeas he should go back home. He hauls everybody down to the equator to grow Northern flowers?"

(10) "It's not just that. Remember how he liked his study back at the house? Well, it's like that, except it's a greenhouse kind of a study."

"Anybody build a greenhouse on the equator ought to be shame."

"This is not the equator."

"Could of fooled me."

(15) "Nowhere near it."

"You mean there's some place on this planet hotter than this?"

"I thought you liked it here."

"Love it."

"Then stop complaining."

(20)   "It's because I do love it that I'm complaining. I'd like to know if
it's permanent. Living like this you can't figure nothing. He might pack
up any minute and trot off someplace else."

     "He'll be here till he dies," Sydney told her. "Less that greenhouse
burns up."

From *Tar Baby* by Toni Morrison.

8. At the beginning of the passage, who first mentions *a shed,*
Sydney or his wife? _____

9. What are *hydrangeas* and *dahlias* (Line 7)?
   (1) greenhouses
   (2) flowers
   (3) tropical birds

10. The word *he* is used three times in Line 8. Who does it refer to?
   (1) Sydney
   (2) Sydney and Ondine's boss
   (3) another worker

11. Who says, *This is not the equator* (Line 13)? _____

12. Who says, *It's because I do love it that I'm complaining*
(Line 20)? _____

13. Which of the following best expresses what the complaint is?
   (1) I don't like the uncertainty about whether we're going to stay
       here.
   (2) It's too hot here.
   (3) The boss is crazy, and he makes me nervous.

Questions 14 to 20 refer to the following poem. It contains a dialogue,
but there are no quotation marks. Even so, the poet has made it easy to
follow. All the words of one character are indented. The words of the
other character are at the left margin of the page.

EARLY EVENING QUARREL
       Where is that sugar, Hammond,
       I sent you this morning to buy?
       I say, where is that sugar
       I sent you this morning to buy?
   (5) Coffee without sugar
       Makes a good woman cry.

<pre>
                    I ain't got no sugar, Hattie,
                    I gambled that dime away.
                    Ain't got no sugar, I
(10)   Done gambled that dime away.
                    If you's a wise woman, Hattie,
                    You ain't gonna have nothing to say.
              I ain't no wise woman, Hammond.
              I am evil and mad.
(15)   Ain't no sense in a good woman
        Being treated so bad.
                    I don't treat you bad, Hattie,
                    Neither does I treat you good.
                    But I reckon I could treat you
(20)   Worser if I would.
              Lawd, these things we women
              Have to stand!
              I wonder is there nowhere a
              Do-right man?
</pre>

From *Selected Poems of Langston Hughes.*

14. Name the two characters in the poem.

    _____ and _____

15. Who speaks first? _____

16. The character who first speaks asks for what? _____

17. What happened to the money? _____

18. After the man confesses what he did, he

    (1) apologizes and asks the woman to forgive him
    (2) tells the woman that, if she's smart, she won't complain
    (3) suggests that the woman express her anger and get it out of her system

19. Who says, *I am evil and mad* (Line 14)? _____

20. In his last speech in the dialogue, the man tells the woman that he

    (1) doesn't treat her so badly
    (2) gives her a lot of treats
    (3) plans to start treating her worse

Check your answers on page 174.

Dialogue in Drama

A drama (a play) is made up mostly of dialogue.

Plays are usually written with the name of the character who is to speak at the beginning of each line. **Stage directions,** or instructions for the actors, are usually written in parentheses ( ) or brackets [ ]. These instructions are not part of the dialogue.

When you read a play, imagine watching actors perform it. Remember that you would not hear their names before each line, and you would not hear the instructions.

TRY THIS

The following passage is from the screenplay for the movie *Driving Miss Daisy* by Alfred Uhry. The screenplay was made from the original play by Mr. Uhry. The characters in this passage are Daisy Werthan, a widow, and Hoke Colburn, her driver. Read the passage and answer the questions that follow.

> [DAISY'S KITCHEN. *Daisy is frying chicken. Hoke enters and watches her.*]
> HOKE: You fixin' to ruin it?
> DAISY: What are you talking about?
> HOKE: You got de skillet turn up too high and de chicken too close together.
> (5) DAISY: Mind your business.
> HOKE: It's yo' chicken. *[He leaves the kitchen. Daisy turns the flame down.]*

What is Daisy doing when Hoke enters? _____

What criticism does Hoke make? _____

What does Daisy tell Hoke after he criticises her? _____

How and when does Daisy react to Hoke's advice? _____

Daisy is frying chicken when Hoke enters.

Hoke tells Daisy that the skillet is too hot and that the chicken is too close together.

Daisy tells Hoke to mind his own business.

Daisy turns down the flame after Hoke leaves.

Notice that the writer tries to show the actors how to speak with a dialect. A dialect is a way of speaking typical of a place or a group.

The writer wants the actor who plays Hoke to say *fixin', de, turn,* and *yo'* instead of *fixing, the, turned,* and *your.*

Read the next passages and answer the questions about them.

Questions 1 to 4 refer to the following passage. It is a dialogue between Dodge and his wife, Halie. Tilden and Bradley are their sons. Dodge is sitting on a sofa watching television. Halie is not on the stage during this scene. That's why her lines begin with *HALIE'S VOICE.*

HALIE'S VOICE: Are you going out today?

DODGE: (*gesturing toward rain*) In this?

HALIE'S VOICE: I'm just asking a simple question.

DODGE: I rarely go out in the bright sunshine. Why should I go out in
(5)   this?

HALIE'S VOICE: I'm just asking because I'm not doing any shopping
    today. And if you need anything you should ask Tilden.

DODGE: Tilden's not here!

HALIE'S VOICE: He's in the kitchen.

(10)   (*Dodge looks toward stage left, then back toward T.V.*)

DODGE: All right.

HALIE'S VOICE: What?

DODGE: (*louder*) All right!

HALIE'S VOICE: Don't scream. It'll only get your coughing started.

(15) DODGE: All right.

From *Buried Child* by Sam Shepard.

1. What is the weather like? _____

2. Who says, *I rarely go out in the bright sunshine?* _____

3. Who explains that Tilden is in the kitchen? _____

4. Why does Dodge feel he has to shout (Line 13) to make Halie hear him?

   (1) Halie is deaf.
   (2) Halie is in another room.
   (3) Halie is not paying attention.

Questions 5 to 10 refer to the following passage from the play *The Odd Couple*. This play was the idea for a popular television series. The two characters in the passage are Felix and Oscar. They are friends with one thing in common. They both recently split up from their wives. This passage takes place in Oscar's apartment. Oscar has told Felix that he can move into the apartment for a while. Felix is cleaning the apartment when they begin to talk.

FELIX: I want to do *something*, Oscar. Let me do something.

OSCAR: [*Nods*] All right, you can take my wife's initials off the towels. Anything you want.

FELIX: [*Beginning to tidy up*] I can cook. I'm a terrific cook.

(5) OSCAR: You don't have to cook. I eat cold cuts for breakfast.

FELIX: Two meals a day at home, we'll save a fortune. We've got to pay alimony, you know.

OSCAR: [*Happy to see Felix's new optimism*] All right, you can cook. [*He throws a pillow at him*]

(10) FELIX: [*Throws the pillow back*] Do you like leg of lamb?

OSCAR: Yes, I like leg of lamb.

FELIX: I'll make it tomorrow night. I'll have to call Frances. She has my big pot.

OSCAR: *Will you forget Frances!* We'll get our own pots. Don't drive me

(15)   crazy before you move in. [*The phone rings. Oscar picks it up quickly*] Hello? Oh, hello, Frances!

FELIX: [*Stops cleaning and starts to wave his arms wildly. He whispers screamingly*] I'm not here! You didn't see me. You don't know where I am. I didn't call. I'm not here. I'm not here.

(20) OSCAR: [*Into the phone*] Yes, he's here.

FELIX: [*Pacing back and forth*] How does she sound? Is she worried? Is she crying? What is she saying? Does she want to speak to me? I don't want to speak to her.

OSCAR: [*Into the phone*] Yes, he is!

(25) FELIX: You can tell her I'm not coming back. I've made up my mind. I've had it there. I've taken just as much as she has. You can tell her for me if she thinks I'm coming back she's got another think coming. Tell her. Tell her.

OSCAR: [*Into the phone*] Yes! Yes, he's fine.

(30) FELIX: Don't tell her I'm fine! You heard me carrying on before. What are you telling her that for? I'm not fine.

OSCAR: [*Into the phone*] Yes, I understand, Frances.

FELIX: [*Sits down next to Oscar*] Does she want to speak to me? Ask her if she wants to speak to me?

(35) OSCAR: [*Into the phone*] Do you want to speak to him?

FELIX: [*Reaches for the phone*] Give me the phone. I'll speak to her.

OCSAR: [*Into the phone*] Oh. You don't want to speak to him.

FELIX: She doesn't want to speak to me?

OSCAR: [*Into the phone*] Yeah, I see. Right. Well, goodbye. [*He hangs up*]

(40) **FELIX:** She didn't want to speak to me?

OSCAR: No!

FELIX: Why did she call?

OSCAR: She wants to know when you're coming over for your clothes. She wants to have the room repainted.

(45) **FELIX:** Oh!

From *The Odd Couple* by Neil Simon

5. Who says, *I want to do something?* _____

6. What does he offer to do? _____

7. What does Felix say he has to get from his wife? _____

8. Who answers the telephone? _____

9. Who is calling? _____

10. How does Felix learn that Frances wants him to pick up his clothes? _____

Check your answers on page 175.

This section of the unit contains readings from literature and commentary on the arts. These readings can help you prepare for the GED in at least two ways. You can use them to
- expand your general knowledge of literature and the arts
- practice the reading skills covered in Unit 1

Directions: Read the passages and answer the questions about them.

Questions 1 to 6 refer to the following passage, which is a dialogue from a short story. Think about the worries of one of the characters.

"I thought we were going to be eight," David said to his wife, Jessie, seeing that she was setting the table for nine.

(5) "Your father," she said.

"Do you really want him to sit with us tonight?"

"Yes, why not? He enjoys a little company."

(10) "I know he enjoys it, but it's embarrassing. He's much better off in his room."

"No, he isn't," she said, and went on setting the table.

(15) "I just hope he doesn't get one of those sneezing attacks. He doesn't know enough to leave the room. And then sometimes he just looks down, his chin against his chest, in a kind of
(20) stupor."

"Oh, not a stupor. Don't make things seem worse than they are. You should talk to him more."

"I think he should stay in bed. He
(25) dishes out his food to whoever's sitting next to him."

"A lot of people do that."

"And he keeps saying the same things all the time."

(30) "So do you," she said, and laughed. "Try to be a little cheerful."

From "At the Dinner Table" by Arturo Vivante.

1. What are the names of the two people in the dialogue? _____ and

   _____

2. Who says, *He enjoys a little company* (Lines 8–9)? _____

3. Throughout the passage, the words *he* and *him* refer to
   (1) the man's father
   (2) the woman's father
   (3) an invited dinner guest

4. Which of the following is NOT one of the objections about the extra person coming to dinner?
   (1) He might get a sneezing attack.
   (2) He eats other people's food.
   (3) He says the same things all the time.

5. Who says, *I think he should stay in bed* (Line 24)? _____

6. At the end of the passage, the woman advises the man
   (1) not to be embarrassed
   (2) to stay in bed
   (3) to try to be a little cheerful

Questions 7 to 10 refer to the following passage about the great jazz singer Billie Holiday. The writer suggests what we should remember about her.

Let us deal here with what will live on as long as there is anything left alive in this culture—her music—and forget for now the rest of it, which
(5) even carried over into graveyard quarrels as to who paid for her tombstone. Billie needs no tombstone, ever. These records—and her others—are a monument to her that
(10) no stone can ever equal. She is in these albums, just as surely as in life, all of her, the good and the bad and the beautiful. It's here in her voice, in the songs and in the titles and the lyrics.
(15) You can't miss it.

I heard her say "baby" once, offstage and not in song. She had opened at a San Francisco nightclub and she was with her then manager, John Levy. She
(20) had waited for Levy to come out of the club and had finally gotten into a car with a group of us. Then he arrived, slipped into the front seat, and she leaned forward and said, "Baaaaaaby,
(25) why did you *leave* me?" In that line was all the **pathos** of "My Man," "Billie's Blues" and the rest. Nobody could say a word for minutes and she didn't even know what she had done.

From record album notes for "The Billie Holiday Story, Volume I" by Ralph J. Gleason.

> *pathos:* pity, sadness

7. Which of the following does the writer think will live on about Billie Holiday?
   (1) her written words
   (2) her music
   (3) the stories about her life

8. What was the quarrel about at her funeral?
   (1) the rights to her records
   (2) her relationship with John Levy
   (3) who would pay for her tombstone

9. The writer says that *Nobody could say a word for minutes* (Lines 27–28) because of
   (1) Billie's anger
   (2) the sadness in Billie's voice
   (3) John Levy's rudeness in being late

10. Which of the following titles best fits the passage?
    (1) Remembering Billie
    (2) Getting Along with Billie
    (3) Understanding Billie's Music

Questions 11 to 14 refer to the following passage from a play. The dialogue takes place in a kitchen. Ella is Emma's mother. Ella is at a stove frying bacon. Emma is carrying hand-painted charts that show the correct way to cut up a frying chicken. Think about why Emma gets angry.

ELLA: What are those things?
EMMA: They're for my demonstration.
ELLA: What demonstration?
EMMA: How to cut up a frying chicken.
(5) ELLA: (*back to bacon*) Oh.
EMMA: For 4–H. You know. I'm giving a demonstration at the fair. I told you before. I hope you haven't used up my last chicken. (*Emma goes to the*
(10) *refrigerator and looks inside for a chicken.*)
ELLA: I forgot you were doing that. I thought that wasn't for months yet.
EMMA: I told you it was this month.
(15) The fair's always this month. Every year it's this month.
ELLA: I forgot.
EMMA: Where's my chicken?
ELLA: (*innocently*) What chicken?
(20) EMMA: I had a fryer in here all ready to go. I killed it and dressed it and everything!
ELLA: It's not in there. All we got is bacon and bread.
(25) EMMA: I just stuck it in here yesterday, Ma! You didn't use it did you?
ELLA: Why would I use it?
EMMA: For soup or something.

ELLA: Why should I use a fryer for
(30) soup? Don't be ridiculous.
EMMA: (*slamming refrigerator*) It's
not in there!
ELLA: Don't start screaming in here!
Go outside and scream if you're
(35) going to scream!

From *Curse of the Starving Class* by Sam Shepard.

11. Near the beginning of the passage,
Emma says she is going to
(1) fry some chicken for her mother
(2) give a demonstration at a fair
(3) cook chicken soup

12. What food is in the house?
(1) soup
(2) bacon and bread
(3) chicken

13. True or false? Ella admits that she has
used Emma's chicken. _____

14. At the end of the passage Ella
(1) helps Emma with her project
(2) leaves the kitchen
(3) tells Emma to go outside if she's
going to scream

Questions 15 to 20 refer to the following
poem, which contains a dialogue. Pay close
attention to who says each line. The poet
has not indented or changed stanzas to indicate a change in speakers.

MADAM AND THE RENT MAN

The rent man knocked.
He said, Howdy-do?
I said, What
Can I do for you?
(5) He said, You know
Your rent is due.

I said, Listen,
Before I'd pay
I'd go to **Hades**
(10) And rot away!

The sink is broke,
The water don't run,
And you ain't done a thing
You promised to've done.

(15) Back window's cracked,
Kitchen floor squeaks,
There's rats in the cellar,
And the attic leaks.

He said, Madam,
(20) It's not up to me.
I'm just the agent,
Don't you see?

I said, Naturally,
You pass the buck.
(25) If it's money you want
You're out of luck.

He said, Madam,
I ain't pleased!
I said, Neither am I.
(30) So we agrees!

From *Selected Poems of Langston Hughes*.

> **Hades:** hell

15. Who is the character who speaks to
Madam? _____

16. Who speaks first? _____

17. In which lines does Madam say she
will not pay the rent? _____

18. Madam complains about each of the
following EXCEPT
(1) a broken sink
(2) a cracked window
(3) the hot water
(4) rats in the cellar

19. Who says, *Naturally, you pass the
buck* (Lines 23–24)? _____

20. Which of the following is the topic of
the poem?
(1) a visit by a stranger
(2) an argument between a tenant and
a rental agent
(3) a description of an old house

Questions 21 to 25 refer to the following passage about eating. The word *culinary* in the first sentence means having to do with cooking.

One of the stupidest things in an earnest but stupid school of culinary thought is that each of the three daily meals should be "balanced."

(5) In the first place, not all people need or want three meals each day. Many of them feel better with two, or one and one-half, or five.

Next, and most important perhaps, (10) "balance" is something that depends entirely on the individual. One man, because of his chemical set-up, may need many proteins. Another, more nervous perhaps, may find meats and (15) eggs and cheeses an active poison, and have to live with what grace he can on salads and cooked squash.

Of course, where countless humans are herded together, as in military (20) camps or schools or prisons, it is necessary to strike what is ironically called the happy medium. In this case what kills the least number with the most ease is the chosen way.

From *How to Cook a Wolf* by M. F. K. Fisher.

21. The writer thinks the idea that each of the three meals a day should be balanced is
    (1) earnest
    (2) wise
    (3) stupid

22. The writer thinks that balance in a person's diet depends on the

    _____.

23. Which of the following means the same as *what kills the least number with the most ease* as used in Lines 23–24?
    (1) food that a large number of people can eat
    (2) food that kills most people
    (3) food that is easy to prepare

24. Which of the following titles best fits this passage?
    (1) The Importance of Three Meals a Day
    (2) What a Balanced Diet Is
    (3) Planning Meals for a Large Number of People

25. Which of the following statements from the passage gives the main idea?
    (1) One of the stupidest things in an earnest but stupid school of culinary thought is that each of the three daily meals should be "balanced." (Lines 1–4)
    (2) "Balance" is something that depends entirely on the individual. (Lines 10–11)
    (3) What kills the least number with the most ease is the chosen way. (Lines 23–24)

Check your answers on page 175.

INTERPRETING LITERATURE AND THE ARTS READINGS 1
SKILLS CHART

To review the reading skills covered by the questions in Interpreting Literature and the Arts Readings 1, study the following parts of Unit 1.

Unit 1 Comprehending What You Read	Item Number
Chapter 1 Finding Details	1, 3, 4, 6, 7, 8, 9, 12, 13, 15, 18, 21, 22, 23
Chapter 2 Finding Topics and Main Ideas	10, 20, 24, 25
Chapter 3 Reading Dialogue	2, 5, 11, 14, 16, 17, 19

INTERPRETING LITERATURE AND THE ARTS READINGS 1
CONTENT CHART

The following chart shows the type of reading passage each item in Interpreting Literature and the Arts Readings 1 refers to.

Type of Literature	Item Number
Nonfiction	21, 22, 23, 24, 25
Fiction	1, 2, 3, 4, 5, 6
Drama	11, 12, 13, 14
Poetry	15, 16, 17, 18, 19, 20
Commentary	7, 8, 9, 10

This section will give you practice at answering questions like those on the GED. The Interpreting Literature and the Arts Test has 45 questions, all multiple choice. Each question has 5 alternatives, or choices. The 10 questions in this Practice are all multiple choice, like the ones on the GED. As on the GED, there is a question before each passage. If you read each passage with that question in mind, it will help you to pay attention to the important details and ideas in the passage.

Directions: Choose the one best answer to each item.

Items 1 to 4 are based on the following passage.

WHAT IS THE DIFFERENCE BETWEEN NEWS AND FICTION?

I am reminded now, as I think about news and fiction, of a demonstration of the difference between noise and melody which I saw and heard in a freshman
(5) physics lecture at Cornell University so long ago. (Freshman physics is invariably the most satisfying course offered by any American university.) The professor threw a narrow board, which was about
(10) the length of a bayonet, at the wall of the room, which was cinder block. "That's noise," he said.
Then he picked up seven more boards, and he threw them against the wall in
(15) rapid succession, as though he were a knife-thrower. The boards in sequence sang the opening notes of "Mary Had a Little Lamb." I was enchanted.
"That's melody," he said.
(20) And fiction is melody, and journalism, new or old, is noise.

From Wampeters, Foma & Granfalloons (Opinions)
by Kurt Vonnegut.

1. The author thinks that a course in freshman physics is
   (1) a good course for learning about fiction
   (2) the most difficult course most students take
   (3) the only course good for learning about news
   (4) the most satisfying course offered in American universities
   (5) a good course for learning about music

2. The author says the professor threw the seven boards as though he were a
   (1) musician
   (2) soldier
   (3) bayonet
   (4) newspaper reporter
   (5) knife-thrower

3. What word does the author use to describe how he felt about the professor's demonstration?
   (1) enchanted
   (2) disbelieving
   (3) doubtful
   (4) angry
   (5) amused

4. Which of the following sentences from the passage best states the main idea of the passage?

    (1) I am reminded now, as I think about news and fiction, of a demonstration of the difference between noise and melody which I saw and heard in a freshman physics lecture at Cornell University so long ago.

    (2) Freshman physics is invariably the most satisfying course offered by any American university.

    (3) The boards in sequence sang the opening notes of "Mary Had a Little Lamb."

    (4) I was enchanted.

    (5) And fiction is melody, and journalism, new or old, is noise.

Items 5 to 7 are based on the following excerpt from a play.

WHY DOES WALTER THINK VICTOR AND ESTHER ARE FORTUNATE PEOPLE?

WALTER: Vic, we were both running from the same thing. I thought I wanted to be tops, but what it was, was untouchable. I ended in a swamp of
(5) success and bankbooks, you on civil service. The difference is that you haven't hurt other people to defend yourself. And I've learned to respect that, Vic; you simply tried to make
(10) yourself useful.

ESTHER: That's wonderful—to come to such an understanding with yourself.

WALTER: Esther, it's a strange thing; in the hospital, for the first time since we
(15) were boys, I began to feel . . . like a brother. In the sense that we shared something. (To Victor): And I feel I would know how to be friends now.

VICTOR: (after a slight pause—he is
(20) unsure): Well, fine. I'm glad of that.

WALTER: (He sees the reserve but feels he has made headway and presses on a bit more urgently): You see, that's why you're still so married. That's a very
(25) rare thing. And why your boy's in such good shape. You've lived a real life. (To Esther): But you know that better than I.

ESTHER: I don't know what I know, Walter.

WALTER: Don't doubt it, dear—believe me,
(30) you're fortunate people. (To Victor): You know that, don't you?

VICTOR: (without looking at Esther): I think so.

ESTHER: It's not quite as easy as you
(35) make it, Walter.

From The Price by Arthur Miller.

5. Which of the following does Walter say is a difference between Victor and himself?

    (1) Victor has been more financially successful.

    (2) Victor respects people more.

    (3) Victor hasn't hurt people.

    (4) Victor has more friends.

    (5) Victor is no longer married.

6. Who says I feel I would know how to be friends now?

    (1) Esther

    (2) Walter

    (3) Victor

    (4) Esther's brother

    (5) Victor's son

7. Walter gives each of the following as a reason for thinking that Victor and Esther are fortunate EXCEPT:

    (1) Victor and Esther are still married.

    (2) Victor and Esther's son is in good shape.

    (3) Victor has lived a real life.

    (4) Victor has ended up on top.

    (5) Victor has tried to make himself useful.

Items 8 to 10 are based on the following excerpt from a novel.

WHAT GIVES COMFORT TO SYDNEY AND ONDINE?

Down below, where the moon couldn't get to, in the servants' quarters, Sydney and Ondine made alternate trips to the bathroom and went quickly back to
(5) sleep. Ondine dreaming of sliding into water, frightened that her heavy legs and swollen ankles will sink her. But still

asleep she turns over and touches her husband's back—the dream dissolves
(10) and with it the anxiety. He is in Baltimore now as usual and because it was always a red city in his mind—red brick, red sun, red necks and cardinals—his dream of it now was rust-colored. Wagons, fruit
(15) stands, all rust-colored. He had left that city to go to Philadelphia and there he became one of those industrious Philadelphia Negroes—the proudest people in the race. That was over fifty
(20) years ago, and still his most vivid dreams were the red rusty Baltimore of 1921. The fish, the trees, the music, the horses' harnesses. It was a tiny dream he had each night that he would never recollect
(25) from morning to morning. So he never knew what it was exactly that refreshed him.

From <u>Tar Baby</u> by Toni Morrison.

8. In the passage, Ondine is frightened about
   (1) working
   (2) sinking
   (3) swimming
   (4) losing her job
   (5) forgetting her childhood

9. To make her anxiety go away, Ondine
   (1) goes for a swim
   (2) walks to the fruit market
   (3) takes a ride on a horse
   (4) touches Sydney's back
   (5) thinks about her hometown

10. The topic of the passage is
    (1) work
    (2) old age
    (3) youth
    (4) dreams
    (5) memory

Check your answers on page 176.

GED PRACTICE 1 SKILLS CHART

To review the reading skills covered by the items in GED Practice 1, study the following parts of Unit 1.

Unit 1 Comprehending What You Read	Item Number
Chapter 1 Finding Details	1, 2, 3, 5, 7, 8, 9
Chapter 2 Finding Topics and Main Ideas	4, 10
Chapter 3 Reading Dialogue	6

GED PRACTICE 1 CONTENT CHART

The following chart shows the type of reading passage each item in GED Practice 1 refers to.

Type of Literature	Item Number
Nonfiction	1, 2, 3, 4
Fiction	8, 9, 10
Drama	5, 6, 7

UNIT 2

Inferring As You Read

This unit is about **inferential comprehension.** Inferential comprehension means understanding what a writer means but does not tell you directly.

In Chapter 1 of this unit, you will make inferences about details that are not stated in passages. You will tell which stated details in a passage you base your inferences on. You will also infer the meanings of certain words in passages. In Chapter 2 you will infer what the main ideas or main purposes of passages are. Also, by using your skill at making inferences, you will draw conclusions from the passages you read.

You read three selections from William Least Heat Moon's nonfiction work *Blue Highways* in Unit 1. You will read part of one of those selections again in this unit.

Unit 2 Overview

1 INFERRING UNSTATED DETAILS

In the first unit of this book, you practiced finding details in a passage. You can use the details you find in a passage to make inferences.

To understand all that a writer means, you must watch for clues. These clues and your knowledge about the world will help you understand more of what a writer tells you. Writers *imply* ideas through details. You can *infer* ideas from writers' details.

Lesson 7

Inferences from Details

In life you make inferences all the time. Suppose you meet a friend in the street. You ask him how he's doing. He answers, "Oh, okay, I guess." Your friend looks tired. He appears not to have shaved for two days, and his shirt isn't ironed.

What do you infer? Your friend hasn't said that anything is wrong. However, his answer, "Oh, okay, I guess," doesn't sound good to you. His appearance is another clue that things are not quite right. You *cannot* infer that your friend had a fight with his wife or that he lost his job or that one of his children is sick. You don't have evidence for any of these specific things. You can, however, infer that something is wrong.

Details in a passage can suggest ideas without actually stating them. For example, if you read that a character has wrinkled skin, you may infer that he is old. If you read that trees are budding, you may infer that the season is spring. If you read that an army battalion is surrounded by enemy forces, you may infer that the battalion is in trouble.

TRY THIS

Read the next passage and pay close attention to the details. Think about the ideas suggested by the details. Then answer the questions that follow.

Mary steers her chair to the desk and turns the pages of a photo album. She smiles when she sees the faded picture of Tom and the children with her on vacation at the beach. Then she remembers the accident that happened a few months after that

(5)   happy trip—the accident that left Mary confined to a chair and the children without a father.

Who is first mentioned in the passage? _____

What two things does the person do in the first sentence? _____ and _____

What word in Line 2 describes the picture? _____

Who is pictured in the photograph? _____

What happened a few months after the vacation? _____

What phrase in Line 5 describes Mary's condition? _____

What phrase in the last line describes the children's condition? _____

You can answer all these questions from details given directly in the passage. The first sentence talks about Mary. In the first sentence, she steers her chair to the desk and turns the pages of a photo album. The picture in Line 2 is faded. Mary, Tom, and the children are pictured in the photograph. An accident happened soon after the vacation. Line 5 says that Mary is confined to a chair. The last line says that the children are without a father.

NOW TRY THIS

You *cannot* answer the following questions directly from details in the passage, but you can infer the answers from the details.

Did the accident happen recently or some time ago? _____ _____

What kind of chair is Mary sitting in? _____

Who was Tom? _____

Tell two things that happened as a result of the accident. _____ and _____

The accident probably happened some time ago. Because the photo Mary looked at was faded, you can infer that it was taken some time ago. The accident occurred only a few months after the vacation, so it must also have happened some time ago.

Mary is probably sitting in a wheelchair. In the first sentence, Mary *steers* her chair. This action suggests a wheelchair. There is another clue in Line 5: Mary is *confined to a chair.*

Tom was probably Mary's husband or the children's father. Again, the passage doesn't tell you. However, it does tell you that Tom was in the vacation picture with Mary and the children. This suggests that he is part of the family.

Probably Tom was killed and Mary was disabled as a result of the accident. The passage suggests that Tom was the children's father, and the last sentence says that the children are without a father. The passage also says the accident left Mary confined to a chair.

Do not try to infer more than a passage suggests. In the passage you just read, for example, you cannot infer Mary's age or her children's ages. You cannot infer how Mary raised the children without their father.

EXERCISE 7

Read each passage and answer the questions that follow. Some of the questions about stated details may help you to answer the inference questions.

Questions 1 to 4 refer to the following paragraph from a short story. Think about the woman's reaction to what she reads.

> My mother read everything except books. Advertisements on buses, entire menus as we ate, billboards; if it had no cover it interested her. So when she found a letter in my drawer that was not addressed to her she read it. "What difference does it make if James has nothing to
> (5) hide?"—that was her thought. She stuffed the letter in the drawer when she finished it and walked from room to room in the big empty house, talking to herself. She took the letter out and read it again to get the facts straight. Then, without putting on her coat or locking the door, she went down the steps and headed for the church at the end of
> (10) the street. No matter how angry and confused she might be, she always went to four o'clock Mass and now it was four o'clock.

From "The Liar" by Tobias Wolff.

1. Name three things that the mother reads. _____, _____, and _____

2. What is the name of the narrator—the person telling the story? _____

3. In Lines 6–7 the narrator says the woman *walked from room to room . . . talking to herself.* These details suggest that the woman is

  (1) crazy
  (2) upset
  (3) searching for something

4. Why did the woman leave *without putting on her coat or locking the door* (Lines 8 and 9)?

  (1) She was careless.
  (2) The weather was warm, and the neighborhood was safe.
  (3) She was upset by what she read in the letter.

Questions 5 to 8 refer to the following paragraph. It is from a memoir about the writer James Agee. A *memoir* tells personal experiences. This memoir was written by a friend and work associate of James Agee.

> He wore blue or khaki work shirts and under the armpits there would be stains, salt-edged, from sweat; likewise under the arms of his suit jacket, double-breasted dark blue, wrinkled and shiny. He was too poor to afford a lot of laundering, and he didn't believe in it, anyway.
>
> (5) After the baby arrived in March, '40, I remember one big scene in which Jim was engaged in spooning **Pablum** into Joel. The father sat, all elbows and knees, in an arm chair upholstered in some ragged and ancient fabric that had grown black absorbing through the years the grime of New York. The infant in his lap mouthed with a will at the
>
> (10) Pablum but inevitably gobs of it splattered down even on the richly unsanitary arms of the chair, whence Jim would scoop it in long dives lest it drip—**irretrievably**, you could hope—on the floor.

From "A Memoir" by Robert Fitzgerald.

Pablum: a brand of baby food
irretrievably: impossible to get back

5. Why did Jim, the man described in the paragraph, wear stained clothes? _____

6. Joel is probably Jim's

  (1) baby
  (2) father
  (3) wife

7. The phrase *all elbows and knees* (Lines 6–7) suggests that the father was

   (1) short and fat
   (2) mean and selfish
   (3) tall and thin

8. The author says *irretrievably, you could hope* in Line 12 because he hoped

   (1) the food would be saved for later
   (2) the father would not feed the baby food that had fallen on the floor
   (3) Jim would leave the spilled food on the arms of the chair

Questions 9 to 13 refer to the following passage. It is from an autobiography, a book about an author's own life. The passage describes an event from the author's childhood.

      It was 1955 and we were driving from Florida to Utah, to get away from a man my mother was afraid of and to get rich on uranium. We were going to change our luck.
      We'd left Sarasota in the dead of summer, right after my tenth
(5) birthday, and headed West under low flickering skies that turned black and exploded and cleared just long enough to leave the air gauzy with steam. We drove through Georgia, Alabama, Tennessee, Kentucky, stopping to cool the engine in towns where people moved with arthritic slowness and spoke in thick, strangled tongues. Idlers with rotten teeth
(10) surrounded the car to press peanuts on the pretty Yankee lady and her little boy, arguing among themselves about shortcuts. Women looked up from their flower beds as we drove past, or watched us from their porches, sometimes impassively, sometimes giving us a nod and a flutter of their fans.

From *This Boy's Life* by Tobias Wolff.

9. Throughout the passage, *we* and *us* refer to

   (1) a husband and wife
   (2) people from Florida and Utah
   (3) a mother and son

10. Give two reasons why the two people were driving to Utah.

   _____ and _____

11. The words *skies that turned black and exploded* (Lines 5–6) suggest that the two people drove west

    (1) mostly at night
    (2) through thunder and lightning
    (3) during a war

12. The phrase *thick, strangled tongues* in Line 9 refers to how people

    (1) talked
    (2) acted
    (3) looked

13. Since people argued *among themselves about shortcuts* (Line 11), the woman had probably asked for

    (1) directions
    (2) peanuts
    (3) flowers

Check your answers on page 177.

Lesson 8

Details that Support Inferences

In the last lesson you learned to make inferences from details in a passage. When you make an inference, check the details to be sure they support your inference.

TRY THIS

Read the following passage and answer the questions that follow it. To answer the first question, you'll need to make an inference.

> Bill knew more about life than when he last walked on this street. He had got out of the army and had finished school. He even had two boys of his own now. Most of the time he felt good about himself. But today he is worried. Would his usually taciturn father
> (5) say anything this time? Or would they sit, again, in angry silence?

Has it been only a few days or a long time since Bill last walked on the street mentioned in Line 2? _____

To support your answer, you need to find details that suggest the passing of time. The passage lists three things that happened to Bill since he last walked on this street. What are they? _____, _____, and _____

Lines 2–3 say that since Bill last walked on the street, he had got out of the army, had finished school, and had two boys of his own. These facts suggest that several years have passed since Bill last walked on the street.

NOW TRY THIS

Reread the passage about Bill and answer the following questions. The first is an inference question.

Is Bill relaxed and happy about what he is going to do? _____

To support your answer, you need to find a detail that tells how Bill feels now. According to the passage, how does Bill feel today?

_____

Line 4 says Bill is worried today. This detail suggests that Bill is not relaxed and happy about what he is going to do.

NOW TRY THIS

Answer the following questions that refer to the passage about Bill. The first is an inference question.

What is Bill about to do? _____

To support your answer, you need to find details that suggest what is about to happen. Who is mentioned for the first time in Line 4?

_____

Who does the word *they* refer to in the last sentence? _____

Bill's father is mentioned for the first time in Line 4. The word *they* refers to Bill and his father. You can infer that Bill is going to visit his father.

EXERCISE 8

Read the next passages and answer the questions that follow them. Some of the questions are simply about details in the passages. Other questions are about details that support inferences, and still other questions ask you to make inferences.

Questions 1 to 5 refer to the following poem by a Chinese poet who lived around the year 1200.

MORNING

I get up. I am sick of
Rouging my cheeks. My face in
The mirror disgusts me. My
Thin shoulders are bowed with
(5) Hopelessness. Tears of loneliness
Well up in my eyes. Wearily
I open my toilet table.
I arch and paint my eyebrows
And steam my heavy braids.
(10) My maid is so stupid that she
Offers me plum blossoms for my hair.

By Chu Shu Chen; from *One Hundred Poems
from the Chinese* by Kenneth Rexroth.

Rouging: putting on color, makeup

1. Who tells the story in the poem?
   (1) an old man
   (2) a young maid
   (3) an old woman
   (4) a gardener

2. According to Line 2, what is the narrator sick of? _____

3. What word describes the narrator's reaction to the face in the mirror? _____

4. The actions described in Lines 8–9 suggest that the narrator is
   (1) a woman
   (2) a man
   (3) a child

5. What do the words *hopelessness, loneliness,* and *wearily* (Lines 5–6) suggest about the age of the narrator? _____

Questions 6 to 10 refer to the following passage from a short story. As you read the passage, look for clues that suggest what the narrator's job is.

I am sitting over coffee and cigarets at my friend Rita's and I am telling her about it.

Here is what I tell her.

It is late of a slow Wednesday when Herb seats the fat man at my
(5) station.

This fat man is the fattest person I have ever seen, though he is neat-appearing and well dressed enough. Everything about him is big. But it is the fingers I remember best. When I stop at the table near his to see to the old couple, I first notice the fingers. They look three times
(10) the size of a normal person's fingers—long, thick, creamy fingers.

I see to my other tables, a party of four businessmen, very demanding, another party of four, three men and a woman, and this old couple. Leander has poured the fat man's water, and I give the fat man plenty of time to make up his mind before going over.

(15) Good evening, I say. May I serve you? I say.

Rita, he was big, I mean big.

Good evening, he says. Hello. Yes, he says. I think we're ready to order now, he says.

He has this way of speaking—strange, don't you know. And he
(20) makes a little puffing sound every so often.

I think we will begin with a Caesar salad, he says. And then a bowl of soup with some extra bread and butter, if you please. The lambchops, I believe, he says. And baked potato with sour cream. We'll see about dessert later. Thank you very much, he says, and hands me
(25) the menu.

God, Rita, but those were fingers.

From "Fat" by Raymond Carver.

6. Where does the narrator work? _____

7. What is the narrator's job? _____

8. Which words and phrases in the following list give clues about what the narrator's job is?

_____ coffee and cigarets (Line 1)

_____ my station (Lines 4 and 5)

_____ the old couple (Line 9)

_____ my other tables (Line 11)

_____ fingers (Lines 8, 9, 10, and 26)

_____ menu (Line 25)

9. The narrator says that the fat man has a strange way of speaking. What is the narrator referring to?

   (1) The fat man orders so much food.
   (2) The fat man makes a puffing sound.
   (3) The fat man refers to himself as "we."

10. What detail about the fat man impresses the narrator most?

   (1) his clothes
   (2) his fingers
   (3) his speech

The Preservation Hall Band playing in New Orleans, *the cradle of jazz.*

Questions 11 to 15 refer to the following paragraph from a commentary written by a jazz critic. The paragraph has many details, but watch for those details that describe the contributions and the character of Jelly Roll Morton.

   In 1938, the pianist, composer, and bandleader Jelly Roll Morton, upset by a Robert Ripley "Believe It or Not" radio program in which W. C. Handy was credited with having invented jazz, sent a long letter to the Baltimore *Afro-American* and to *down beat* saying, "It is
(5) evidently known, beyond contradiction, that New Orleans is the cradle of *jazz,* and I, myself, happened to be the creator in the year 1902." Morton was a famous braggart, and the letter was hooted down; everybody knew—or thought he knew—that Morton had not done anything important in jazz until the mid-twenties, when he recorded
(10) with his Red Hot Peppers. But **hyperbole** often dances on fact. Twenty

years after Morton wrote his letter, the **stride pianist** and composer James P. Johnson told an interviewer named Tom Davin that he had heard Morton at Barron Wilkins' club in New York in 1911. Morton "had just arrived from the West and he was red hot," Johnson said.

(15) "The place was on fire." So Morton may well have been playing some sort of jazz around 1902, and Johnson himself, with his Harlem **confreres** the pianists Luckey Roberts and Willie the Lion Smith, was probably playing a music akin to jazz not long after Morton came through town. All of which is to say that jazz pianists, extracting the

(20) choicest juice from ragtime, did help to invent jazz; and when the music has been struck by fads or **fickleness** they have preserved its lyrical essence. They have also been invaluable composers, leaders, and teachers; pianists taught the strange augmented chords of bebop to the young trumpeters and saxophonists of the early forties.

From "Keepers of the Flame" by Whitney Balliett.

hyperbole: exaggeration
stride pianist: a jazz piano player who keeps a steady beat with his left hand
confreres: colleagues, associates
fickleness: change in interests, change in loyalties

11. It is probably true that Jelly Roll Morton

   (1) never told the truth
   (2) created jazz piano playing in New Orleans in 1902
   (3) was playing something like jazz in the early 1900s

12. What did Morton claim in his 1938 letter to *Afro-American?*

   (1) that Harlem was the birthplace of jazz
   (2) that he had created jazz
   (3) that jazz was created in 1938

13. Why was the letter *hooted down,* as Line 7 says?

   (1) Morton had a reputation for bragging.
   (2) People knew who had really invented jazz.
   (3) People were sure Morton's jazz contributions were in the thirties.

14. Which of the following means the same as the sentence, *But hyperbole often dances on fact* (Line 10)?

   (1) Modern dance and jazz are closely related.
   (2) Truth is stranger than fiction.
   (3) An exaggeration can have an element of truth.

15. The author would NOT agree that

    (1) pianists have made important contributions to jazz
    (2) the date and place of the invention of jazz is finally known
    (3) musicians in Harlem were playing something like jazz in the early 1900s

Check your answers on page 177.

Lesson 9

Word Meanings

It is useful to have a dictionary to look up new words you find. However, you can't always have a dictionary with you. The context that an unfamiliar word appears in can sometimes help you figure out the meaning of a word you don't know. This is another example of making an inference. You use the clues in the details around a new word to figure out the meaning.

TRY THIS

Read this part of the paragraph about Bill you studied in Lesson 8. Then try to infer the meaning of the word *taciturn.*

> But today he is worried. Would his usually taciturn father say anything? Or would they sit, again, in angry silence?

A person who is *taciturn* probably
(1) stays in a good mood most of the time
(2) complains a lot
(3) talks very little

Bill wonders whether his father will say something or sit again in angry silence. These clues suggest that a taciturn person talks very little, Choice (3).

EXERCISE 9

Read each passage and answer the questions about them. Some of the questions about details in the passages will help you discover the meanings of words.

Questions 1 and 2 refer to the following passage from a short story. You read this passage before in Lesson 3.

It's so hard to be nice to people. It's something you have to learn. I try to be nice, but it's complicated. You start feeling guilty for your own failures of generosity at just about the same point in life when you start feeling angry, even less willing to give. The two feelings collide—feeling
(5) gracious and feeling mean.

From "With Jazz" by Bobbie Ann Mason.

1. The author thinks we start to feel guilty about not being generous at the same time that we start to
   (1) accept other people more
   (2) forgive and forget
   (3) feel angry and unwilling to give

2. The word *collide* in Line 4 probably means
   (1) fight each other
   (2) are the same
   (3) work together

Question 3 refers to the following passage from an essay.

I don't mean to brag about **family lineage**, but I had an uncle, dead some years now, who had fully two sobriquets: in some quarters he was known as Lefty and in others as Square Sam.

From "Confessions of a Low Roller" by Joseph Epstein.

family lineage: ancestors, relatives

3. The word *sobriquets* in Line 2 probably means
   (1) nicknames
   (2) jobs
   (3) houses

Question 4 refers to the following passage from a book about the author's father.

I listen for my father and I hear a **stammer**. This was explosive and unashamed, not a choking on words but a spray of words. His speech was headlong, edgy, breathless: there was neither room in his mouth nor time in the day to contain what he burned to utter.

From *The Duke of Deception* by Geoffrey Wolff.

stammer: a speaking problem involving uncontrolled stopping and repeating

4. Another word for *utter* in Line 4 is

(1) eat
(2) take
(3) say

Question 5 refers to the following passage from a novel. You read the paragraph this passage comes from in Lesson 1.

Macon had no imperfection and age seemed to strengthen him. Milkman feared his father, respected him, but knew, because of the leg, that he could never emulate him. So he differed from him as much as he dared.

From *The Song of Solomon* by Toni Morrison.

5. The word *emulate* probably means

(1) insult
(2) equal or be like
(3) understand

Questions 6 and 7 refer to the following passage. You read the paragraph the passage comes from in Lesson 1.

The bristlecone pine of American Indians, Hopis live where almost nothing else will, thriving long in adverse conditions: poor soil, drought, temperature extremes, high winds. Those give life to the bristlecone and the Hopi.

From *Blue Highways* by William Least Heat Moon.

6. The writer says that the Hopis live

(1) where plants and animals grow easily
(2) where most things cannot live
(3) where conditions are ideal

7. The word *adverse* in Line 2 probably means

(1) comfortable
(2) warlike
(3) difficult

Questions 8 and 9 refer to the following passage from a humorous book about the writer's travels.

I might have seen more of America when I was a child if I hadn't had to spend so much of my time protecting my half of the back seat from incursions by my sister, Sukey. In the years just after the Second World War, when Sukey and I happened to be at our most territorial,
(5) our family was out on the road for five or six weeks every summer.

From "Travels with Sukey" by Calvin Trillin.

8. The word *incursions* in Line 3 probably means

   (1) gifts
   (2) invasions
   (3) insults

9. *Territorial* in Line 4 probably means

   (1) open to new experiences
   (2) willing to share
   (3) protective of private space

Questions 10 to 12 refer to the following poem. Its meaning depends on one important but uncommon word. Try to infer the meaning from the rest of the poem. The questions that follow the poem should help you figure out the meaning of the unfamiliar word.

THE HOUND
Life the hound
Equivocal
Comes at a **bound**
Either to **rend** me
(5) Or to befriend me.
I cannot tell
The hound's intent
Till he has sprung
At my bare hand
(10) With teeth or tongue.
Meanwhile I stand
And wait the event.

By Robert Francis.

> **bound:** jump
> **rend:** split or tear apart

10. In Lines 1–5 the poet says that life, or the hound, comes with two possibilities. What are they?

   (1) to stay with him or to leave him
   (2) to make him rich or to make him poor
   (3) to tear him apart or to make friends with him

11. The poet says that he will not know the intentions of the hound until the hound

   (1) jumps at him
   (2) looks into his eyes
   (3) leaves

12. The word *equivocal*, as it is used in Line 2, describes something that is

   (1) definite
   (2) uncertain
   (3) evil

Check your answers on page 178.

2 INFERRING IDEAS AND DRAWING CONCLUSIONS

Reading literature can be like solving a mystery. Writers often give clues rather than stating their intentions directly. As you gather more and more clues from a passage, the solution to the mystery becomes clearer. One of the pleasures—and challenges—of reading is using clues to discover writers' ideas.

Lesson 10

Main Ideas and Main Purposes

In Lessons 3 and 4 you learned to identify the topic of a passage and to find the sentence that states the main idea about the topic.

Writers do not always state their main ideas directly. Sometimes you must use clues from a passage to infer the main idea or to find the main point a writer makes.

Passages from fiction—and from some nonfiction, for that matter—don't always have a main idea. Often they have a **main purpose.** For example, the main purpose of a passage may be to show something about a character or to tell how an event occurred.

As you read a passage, especially a passage of fiction, pay attention to how characters are described. Watch for clues that suggest what has happened and what is about to happen. Think about what the details in a passage reveal about its topic. These clues suggest what the author wants to emphasize. They will help you infer what the author's main idea or main purpose is.

TRY THIS

Read the next passage, which comes from a short story. Then answer the questions that follow it. Think about what is about to happen. Think about what the woman is doing and why.

Saturday afternoon the mother drove to the bakery in the shopping center. After looking through a loose-leaf binder with photographs of cakes taped onto the pages, she ordered chocolate, the child's favorite. The cake she chose was decorated with a spaceship and a launching

(5) pad under a sprinkling of white stars. The name SCOTTY would be iced on in green as if it were the name of the spaceship.

The baker listened thoughtfully when the mother told him Scotty would be eight years old. He was an older man, this baker, and he wore a curious apron, a heavy thing with loops that went under his

(10) arms and around his back and then crossed in front again where they were tied in a very thick knot. He kept wiping his hands on the front of the apron as he listened to the woman, his wet eyes examining her lips as she studied the samples and talked.

He let her take her time. He was in no hurry.

(15) The mother decided on the spaceship cake, and then she gave the baker her name and her telephone number. The cake would be ready Monday morning, in plenty of time for the party Monday afternoon. This was all the baker was willing to say. No pleasantries, just this small exchange, the barest information, nothing that was not necessary.

From "The Bath" by Raymond Carver.

Who is Scotty? _____

What is going to happen on Monday afternoon? _____

In this passage the author's main purpose is to tell about
  (1) a mother's shopping trip for a birthday cake for her son
  (2) a baker who doesn't talk much
  (3) the cake the mother decided to order

The passage does not say directly who Scotty is, but you learn that the name SCOTTY will be on the cake, and later (in Line 8) the mother tells the baker that Scotty will be eight years old. You can infer that Scotty is the woman's son.

In the last paragraph you learn that there will be a party on Monday afternoon. You can infer that the party is for Scotty's birthday.

Both Choice (2) and Choice (3) are mentioned in the passage, but they do not represent the main purpose. The author tells about a baker who does not talk much, and he also tells about the birthday cake. However, these descriptions are secondary details that provide background to the author's main purpose of telling about the mother's shopping trip for her son's birthday cake, Choice (1).

EXERCISE 10

Read the next passages and answer the questions that follow them. Some of the questions are detail and inference questions that will help you find the main purpose or main idea.

Questions 1 to 6 refer to the following paragraph from a book about a writer's travels. Think about the differences between the writer and the other person described in the paragraph.

I have a friend in Scotland, a painter, who still lives in the fishing town he was born in, grew up in, went to school in, was married in, raised his children in, works in, and clearly intends to die in. I look on him with uncomprehending awe, for although I had much the same
(5) origins that he had, born and sprouting in rural Scotland, close to the sea, living more by the **agrarian round** than by outside time, I had in my head from an early age the firm notion of leaving, long before I knew why or how. Even less did I realize then that I would come to restless rest in a **whole slew** of places, countries, and languages—the
(10) shifting opposite of my rooted friend. Walking with him through his parish, I am aware that the buildings and trees are as familiar to him as his own fingernails; that the people he throws a passing word to he has known, in all their changings, over a span of some fifty years; that he has surrounding him his own history and the history of the place, in
(15) memory and image, in language and stone; that his past is ever present to him, whereas my own is lost, shed. He has made his peace with place in a way that to me is, if not unimaginable, at least by now beyond me.

From *Whereabouts* by Alastair Reid.

agrarian round: farming routine
whole slew: large number

1. Most of the paragraph is about

   (1) the hardships of travel
   (2) the writer's friend
   (3) a changing village

2. The word *awe* in Line 4 probably means

   (1) pity
   (2) embarrassment
   (3) wonder

3. The sentence that begins, *Even less did I realize . . .*
   (Lines 8–10), suggests that the author

   (1) has finally come back to his homeland
   (2) has remained in his homeland all his life
   (3) has lived and traveled in many places

4. In Lines 9–10, the phrase, *the shifting opposite*, refers to the author's

    (1) traveling all his life
    (2) ability to speak many languages
    (3) changeable moods

5. In the passage, the author implies that he

    (1) could never have lived as his friend has
    (2) feels sorry for his friend because of the way his friend has lived
    (3) is sorry he did not choose to live as his friend has

6. Which of the following best expresses the author's main point?

    (1) He knew when he was young that he wanted to travel.
    (2) He has lived a life of moving and changing while his friend has stayed in one place.
    (3) He cannot understand why his friend chose to stay where he was born.

Questions 7 to 10 refer to the following passage from an essay. Think about the message the author is trying to get across.

A friend of mine has an electric fence around a piece of his land, and keeps two cows there. I asked him one day how he liked his fence and whether it cost much to operate. "Doesn't cost a damn thing," he replied. "As soon as the battery ran down I unhooked it and never put it back.

(5) That strand of fence wire is as dead as a piece of string, but the cows don't go within ten feet of it. They learned their lesson the first few days."

Apparently this state of affairs is general throughout the United States. Thousands of cows are living in fear of a strand of wire that no longer has the power to confine them. Freedom is theirs for the asking.

(10) Rise up, cows! Take your liberty while **despots** snore. And rise up too, all people in bondage everywhere! The wire is dead, the trick is exhausted. Come on out!

From "Poetry" by E. B. White.

> *despots:* rulers with total power; rulers who use their power abusively

7. Why did the author's friend never replace the battery for the electric fence?

   (1) He knew the cows continued to think they would get shocked.
   (2) He wanted the cows to be free.
   (3) He was afraid the cows would get hurt.

8. The words *in bondage* in Line 11 probably mean

   (1) on farms
   (2) without liberty
   (3) with freedom

9. The passage is about

   (1) things that seem confining
   (2) electric fences
   (3) farm problems

10. Which of the following best states the author's message?

    (1) Do as authorities tell you.
    (2) Break away from whatever you think imprisons you.
    (3) Accept your limitations and live with them as happily as you can.

Questions 11 to 15 refer to the following passage from a reminiscence—a telling of an experience. Think about the main character in the passage and about that character's disability.

She remembers the Canadian summer nights when her father used to wrap her in a blanket and take her out to the lake's edge to see the stars.

But she can't dice an onion. She can't set the table. She can't play cards. Her grandson is five, and when they play pairs with his animal

(5) cards, he knows where the second penguin will be. She just turns up cards at random.

He hits her because she can't remember anything, because she keeps telling him not to run around quite so much.

(10) Then I punish him. I tell him he has to understand.

He goes down on the floor, kisses her feet and promises not to hit her again.

She smiles at him, as if for the first time, and says, "Oh, your kiss is so full of sugar."

(15) After a week with him, she looks puzzled and says, "He's a nice little boy. Where does he sleep? I mean, who does he belong to?"

"He's your grandson."

"I see." She looks away and puts her hand to her face.

From "Deficits" by Michael Ignatieff.

11. **Who is the main character in the passage?**

    (1) a five-year-old boy

    (2) a grandmother

    (3) the narrator

12. **Who is most likely the narrator of the story?**

    (1) the little boy

    (2) the grandmother

    (3) the little boy's parent

    (4) a friend of the family

13. **The woman in the story has no trouble**

    (1) recalling her childhood

    (2) slicing onions

    (3) setting the table

    (4) playing cards

14. **The little boy hits the woman because she**

    (1) punishes him

    (2) forgets things

    (3) plays cards

15. **The author's main purpose is to tell about**

    (1) an old woman's loss of memory

    (2) the impatience of a small child

    (3) the problems of the generation gap

Check your answers on page 178.

Conclusions

Sometimes a passage contains so many clues, so much evidence about something, that you can draw some clear **conclusions**. A conclusion is a strong, broad inference. A simple inference is often based on just one detail, and it may give you only a small piece of information. A conclusion, on the other hand, is usually based on several details, and it may give you a broad understanding of something.

TRY THIS

Read the following paragraph from a short story. Think about all the details that describe the relationship between Anderson and his mother. Then answer the questions. In the last question, see if you can draw a conclusion about the characters.

Anderson sat in the airport lounge in Idaho Falls, reading a technical report and waiting anxiously for his mother's plane to land. Around him, a few country people dressed in cotton Western shirts and denim were sipping Cokes, and one of them remarked rather
(5) loudly that the incoming flight had been delayed. So Anderson exchanged his glass of club soda for a bourbon-and-water. He did this with some hesitation, because his mother was a devout Baptist and the slightest tendency toward excess brought a scowl to her face. He had not seen her for almost five years, since an unfortunate scene at
(10) his father's funeral, and he was hoping this time not to offend her, to prove himself worthy of her love.

From "Where the Mountains Are" by Bill Barich.

As Anderson waited for his mother's plane, he felt
(1) cheerful
(2) angry
(3) anxious

He hesitated to drink a bourbon-and-water because
(1) his mother did not like excess
(2) he preferred Coke
(3) his mother would want him to wait until she could join him for a drink

The scene at his father's funeral is described as _____.

What two things does Anderson hope for in the last sentence?

_____ and _____

What can you conclude about the relationship between Anderson and his mother?

> (1) Things have been bad in the past, but both of them are going to try to make things better.
> (2) Their relationship has been bad for five years, and Anderson is worried about seeing his mother.
> (3) The love between Anderson and his mother is unshaken.

Anderson waited anxiously for his mother's plane, Choice (3). He hesitated to get a drink because his mother did not like excess, Choice (1). The scene at the funeral was unfortunate. Anderson hoped not to offend his mother and to prove that he deserved her love.

These details all point to the conclusion in Choice (2). The first conclusion is wrong because there are no clues that suggest the mother's thoughts about meeting her son. The third conclusion is wrong because the love between them *was* shaken. Anderson wants to prove that he is worthy of her love.

EXERCISE 11

Read the next passages and answer the questions that follow them. Some of the questions are about details that can help you draw conclusions.

Questions 1 to 5 refer to the following paragraph from a book about travel. Think about the comparisons the writer makes.

> Trains are for meditation, for playing out long thought-processes, over and over; we trust them, perhaps because they have no choice but to go where they are going. Nowadays, however, they smack of a dying **gentility.** To travel by car makes journeys less mysterious, too much a
> (5) matter of the will. One might as easily sit on a sofa and imagine a passing landscape. I doubt whether any truly absorbing conversation ever took place in a car; they are good only for word games and long, tedious **narratives.** We have come to regard cars too much as appendages of our bodies and will probably pay for it in the end by
> (10) losing the use of our legs. We owe to them the cluttering of the landscape, the breakup of villages and towns.

From *Whereabouts* by Alastair Reid.

| **gentility:** the appearance of social superiority |
| **narratives:** stories |

1. What is the topic of the paragraph?

   (1) good conversation
   (2) train and car travel
   (3) the breakup of society

2. Which of the following is an example of *appendages,* as the word is used in Line 9?

   (1) trains
   (2) stories
   (3) legs
   (4) wheels

3. The author believes that cars are responsible for each of the following EXCEPT

   (1) taking the mystery out of travel
   (2) inspiring good conversation
   (3) cluttering the landscape
   (4) helping to destroy towns

4. The author compares riding in cars to

   (1) having a long conversation
   (2) sitting on a sofa
   (3) playing word games

5. You can conclude from the paragraph that the author

   (1) prefers trains to cars
   (2) appreciates cars for making modern life more convenient
   (3) thinks trains are too old-fashioned
   (4) thinks we do not use cars to their full advantage

Questions 6 to 10 refer to the following passage from a short story about Peter, a divorced father.

On that day, a long Saturday at the beach, when he had all day felt peace and father-love and sun and salt water, he had understood why now in summer he and his children were as he had yearned for them to be in winter: they were no longer confined to car or buildings to remind them
(5) why they were there. The long beach and the sea were their lawn; the blanket their home; the ice chest and thermos their kitchen. They lived as a family again. While he ran and David dug in the sand until he reached water and Kathi looked for pretty shells for her room, the blanket waited for them. It was the place they wandered back to: for food, for drink, for
(10) rest, their talk as casual as between children and father arriving, through separate doors, at the kitchen sink for water, the refrigerator for an

orange. Then one left for the surf; another slept in the sun, lips stained with grape juice. He had wanted to tell the children about it, but it was too much to tell, and the beach was no place for such talk anyway, and he also

(15) guessed they knew. So that afternoon when they were all lying on the blanket, on their backs, the children flanking him, he simply said: 'Divorced kids go to the beach more than married ones.'

'Why?' Kathi said.

'Because married people do chores and errands on weekends. No

(20) kid-days.'

'I love the beach,' David said.

'So do I,' Peter said.

He looked at Kathi.

'You don't like it, huh?'

(25) She took her arm from her eyes and looked at him. His urge was to turn away. She looked at him for a long time; her eyes were too tender, too wise, and he wished she could have learned both later, and differently; in her eyes he saw the car in winter, heard its doors closing and closing, their talk and the sounds of heater and engine and tires on

(30) the road, and the places the car took them. Then she held his hand, and closed her eyes.

'I wish it was summer all year round,' she said.

From "The Winter Father" by Andre Dubus.

6. The writer compares the blanket at the beach to

   (1) a home
   (2) a sofa
   (3) a tent

7. Who are Kathi and David?

   (1) Peter's wife and friend
   (2) Peter's parents
   (3) Peter's children

8. *Divorced kids* in Line 17 means

   (1) couples who divorced when they were very young
   (2) children whose parents are divorced
   (3) Kathi and David's friends

9. *Both* in Line 27 refers to

   (1) Kathi's eyes
   (2) tenderness and wisdom
   (3) Kathi and David

10. Which of the following can you conclude from the passage?

    (1) Both the children and their father like winter sports.

    (2) The children never learned to appreciate their father.

    (3) The divorced father was not comfortable with his children.

    (4) Both the children and their father were happier with each other in the summer.

Questions 11 to 15 refer to the following passage from a play. This scene is a dialogue between the mother, Amanda, and her son, Tom.

AMANDA: I remember suggesting that it would be nice for your sister if you brought home some nice young man from the warehouse. I think that I've made that suggestion more than once.

TOM: Yes, you have made it repeatedly.

(5) AMANDA: Well?

TOM: We are going to have one.

AMANDA: *What?*

TOM: A gentleman caller!

AMANDA: You mean you have asked some nice young man to come over?

(10) TOM: Yep. I've asked him to dinner.

AMANDA: You really did?

TOM: I did!

AMANDA: You did, and did he—*accept?*

TOM: He did!

(15) AMANDA: Well, well—well, well! That's—lovely!

TOM: I thought that you would be pleased.

AMANDA: It's definite, then?

TOM: Very definite.

AMANDA: Soon?

(20) TOM: Very soon.

AMANDA: For heaven's sake, stop putting on and tell me some things, will you?

TOM: What things do you want me to tell you?

AMANDA: *Naturally* I would like to know when he's *coming!*

(25) TOM: He's coming tomorrow.

AMANDA: *Tomorrow?*

TOM: Yep. Tomorrow.

AMANDA: But, Tom!

TOM: Yes, Mother?

(30) AMANDA: Tomorrow gives me no time!

TOM: Time for what?

AMANDA: Preparations! Why didn't you phone me at once, as soon as you asked him, the minute that he accepted? Then, don't you see, I could have been getting ready!

(35) TOM: You don't have to make any fuss.

AMANDA: Oh, Tom, Tom, Tom, of course I have to make a fuss! I want things nice, not sloppy! Not thrown together. I'll certainly have to do some fast thinking, won't I?

TOM: I don't see why you have to think at all.

(40) AMANDA: You just don't know. We can't have a gentleman caller in a pig-sty! All my wedding silver has to be polished, the monogrammed table linen ought to be laundered! The windows have to be washed and fresh curtains put up. And how about clothes? We have to *wear* something, don't we?

(45) TOM: Mother, this boy is no one to make a fuss over!

AMANDA: Do you realize he's the first young man we've introduced to your sister? It's terrible, dreadful, disgraceful that poor little sister has never received a single gentleman caller!

From *The Glass Menagerie* by Tennessee Williams.

11. According to the first two speeches in the passage, what has Amanda asked Tom several times to do?

   (1) to help more with the housework
   (2) to invite a man to dinner
   (3) to get another job

12. When does Tom say that the guest is coming?

   (1) the next day
   (2) in a few days
   (3) in a few weeks

13. Which of the following best describes Amanda's reaction when she learns when the guest is coming?

   (1) relief
   (2) anxiety
   (3) anger

14. Why has Amanda asked Tom to bring *home some nice young man from the warehouse*?

   (1) to introduce Tom's sister to a man
   (2) to show off the new furniture
   (3) to make her children's friends feel welcome

15. **What can you conclude about Amanda's and Tom's feelings about the visit of a gentleman caller?**

    (1) Amanda and Tom agree that the visit is important for Tom's sister.

    (2) Neither Amanda nor Tom thinks the visit is important.

    (3) Amanda thinks the visit is very important, but Tom thinks it's not a big deal.

Check your answers on page 179.

This section of the unit contains readings from literature and commentary on the arts. These readings can help you prepare for the GED in at least two ways. You can use them to

- expand your general knowledge of literature and the arts
- practice the reading skills covered in Units 1 and 2

Directions: Read the passages and answer the questions about them.

Questions 1 to 5 refer to the following passage from a short story. Think about the contrast between the attitudes of the characters.

Shane got arrested just before his sixteenth birthday. It was a dumb bust, out on a suburban street corner in Anaheim, California, on a warm spring
(5) night. A couple of cops were cruising through the haze and saw some kids passing around a joint, and they pulled over and did some unwarranted pushing and shoving, which resulted in
(10) a minor-league riot. Shane did not hit either of the cops, although they testified to the contrary in court, but he did break the antenna of their patrol car, so the judge was not entirely wrong
(15) to give him a suspended sentence and six months' probation. The whole affair was no big deal to Shane, since he didn't feel guilty about what he'd done—the cops had been *asking* for trouble—but
(20) it bothered his grandparents, with whom he'd been living for some time.
His grandfather, Charlie Harris, drove him home after the court appearance. Harris was a retired
(25) phone-company executive, stocky and white-haired, who had great respect for the institutions of the world. "I hope you know how lucky you are to get off easy," he said. "The judge
(30) could have thrown the book at you."
Shane was slumped in his seat, studying his fingernails. "It was a farce."
"You take that kind of attitude and
(35) you'll wind up in the penitentiary."

"I'm not going to wind up in any penitentiary. Anyhow, the cops didn't tell the truth."
"Then they must have had a
(40) reason," Harris said.

From "Hard to Be Good" by Bill Barich.

1. Who is Charlie Harris?
   (1) a policeman
   (2) Shane's grandfather
   (3) a judge

2. The words *had great respect for the institutions of the world* (Lines 26–27) suggest that Mr. Harris
   (1) knew his grandson was right
   (2) probably always trusted authority figures
   (3) had a low-level job

3. The phrase *slumped in his seat* (Line 31) suggests that Shane
   (1) did not care about what was going on
   (2) had a bad back
   (3) was paying close attention to everything around him

4. According to the passage, Shane's sentence was justifiable because he
   (1) hit a policeman
   (2) stole a car
   (3) broke the antenna of a police car

5. The main purpose of the passage is to show that Shane

   (1) had little respect for authority, and his arrest had not changed him
   (2) has learned a lesson and will probably stay out of trouble in the future
   (3) does not respect his grandfather's opinions

Questions 6 to 10 refer to the following paragraph from a memoir about the writer James Agee. It is written by a friend with whom he worked in New York City.

The office building where we worked presented on the ground floor one of the first of those showrooms, enclosed in **convex,** non-reflecting plate glass,
(5) in which a new automobile revolved slowly on a turntable. On Sunday a vacant stillness overcame this exhibition. The building bore the same name as the automobile. It had been
(10) erected in the late 20's as a monument to the car, the engineer and the company, and for a time it held the altitude record until the Empire State Building went higher. It terminated
(15) aloft in a glittering spearpoint of metal **sheathing.** From the fifty-second and fiftieth floors where Agee and I respectively had offices, you looked down on the narrow **cleft**
(20) of Lexington Avenue and across at the Grand Central Building, or you looked north or south over the city or across the East River toward Queens. As a boom-time skyscraper it had more
(25) generous stories than later structures of the kind, higher ceilings, an airier interior. Office doors were frosted in the old-fashioned way, **prevalent** when natural daylight still had value
(30) with designers. In a high wind at our altitude you could feel the sway of the building, a calculated yielding of structural steel. Thus contact of a sort was maintained with weather and the
(35) physical world.

From "A Memoir" by Robert Fitzgerald.

> **convex:** curved
> **sheathing:** covering
> **cleft:** an opening, a crack
> **prevalent:** widespread

6. The paragraph is about

   (1) an office building
   (2) New York City
   (3) an automobile showroom

7. The word *revolved* in Line 5 probably means

   (1) disappeared
   (2) turned
   (3) opened

8. The building the author worked in had each of the following advantages over newer buildings EXCEPT FOR

   (1) more stories
   (2) higher ceilings
   (3) better air-conditioning
   (4) more natural light

9. The sentence that begins *Office doors were frosted in the old-fashioned way* (Lines 27–30) suggests that

   (1) the building was cold in the winter
   (2) there was nothing modern about the building
   (3) building designers today do not make enough use of natural light

10. The words *the sway* in Line 31 refer to

    (1) the movement of the building
    (2) the sound of the wind
    (3) the texture of the steel

Questions 11 to 15 refer to the following paragraph from a short story. There is no real action in the paragraph. Instead, you read the writer's reflections.

Sometimes, when I see people like Rose, I imagine them as babies, as young children. I suppose many of us do. We search the aging skin of the
(5) face, the unhappy eyes and mouth. Of course I can never imagine their fat little faces at the breast, or their cheeks flushed and eyes brightened from play. I do not think of them after
(10) the age of five or six, when they are sent to kindergartens, to school.

There, beyond the shadows of their families and neighborhood friends, they enter the world a second time,
(15) their eyes blinking in the light of it. They will be loved or liked or disliked, even hated; some will be ignored, others singled out for daily abuse that, with a few adult exceptions, only
(20) children have the energy and heart to inflict. Some will be corrupted, many without knowing it, save for that cooling **quiver** of conscience when they cheat, when they lie to save
(25) themselves, when out of fear they side with bullies or teachers, and so forsake loyalty to a friend. Soon they are small men and women, with our sins and virtues, and by the age of
(30) thirteen some have our vices too.

From "Rose" by Andre Dubus.

> *quiver:* shaking, trembling

11. Seeing people like Rose makes the narrator wonder how they
    (1) looked as children
    (2) will look as old people
    (3) look to other people

12. According to the narrator, people *enter the world a second time* (Line 14) when they
    (1) are babies
    (2) turn thirteen
    (3) go to school

13. The narrator thinks that children support bullies and teachers because of
    (1) fear
    (2) conscience
    (3) loyalty

14. The word *forsake* in Line 27 probably means
    (1) promise
    (2) express
    (3) give up

15. The main idea of the paragraph is that
    (1) children are more often abused by other children than by adults
    (2) influences at school play a large part in shaping people's characters
    (3) some children are corrupted without knowing it

Questions 16 to 20 refer to the following passage, another scene in the play *The Glass Menagerie*. In this scene the daughter, Laura, is talking to the gentleman caller, Jim.

JIM: When did you recognize me?
LAURA: Oh, right away!
JIM: Soon as I came in the door?
LAURA: When I heard your name I
(5) thought it was probably you. I knew that Tom used to know you a little in high school. So when you came in the door—Well, then I was—sure.
JIM: Why didn't you *say* something,
(10) then?
LAURA: [*breathlessly*]. I didn't know what to say, I was—too surprised!
JIM: For goodness' sakes! You know, this sure is funny!
(15) LAURA: Yes! Yes, isn't it, though . . .
JIM: Didn't we have a class in something together?
LAURA: Yes, we did.
JIM: What class was that?
(20) LAURA: It was—singing—Chorus!
JIM: Aw!
LAURA: I sat across the aisle from you in the Aud.
JIM: Aw.
(25) LAURA: Mondays, Wednesdays and Fridays.
JIM: Now I remember—that you always came in late.
LAURA: Yes, it was so hard for me,
(30) getting upstairs. I had that brace on my leg—it clumped so loud!
JIM: I never heard any clumping.
LAURA: [*wincing at the recollection*]. To me it sounded like—thunder!
(35) JIM: Well, well, well, I never even noticed.
LAURA: And everybody was seated before I came in. I had to walk in front of all those people. My seat
(40) was in the back row. I had to go

clumping all the way up the aisle
with everyone watching!

JIM: You shouldn't have been
self-conscious.

(45) LAURA: I know, but I was. It was
always such a relief when the
singing started.

JIM: Aw, yes, I've placed you now! I
used to call you Blue Roses. How was
(50) it that I got started calling you that?

LAURA: I was out of school a little while
with pleurosis. When I came back you
asked me what was the matter. I said
I had pleurosis—you thought I said
(55) Blue Roses. That's what you always
called me after that!

JIM: I hope you didn't mind.

LAURA: Oh, no—I liked it. You see, I
wasn't acquainted with
(60) many—people. . . .

JIM: As I remember you sort of stuck
by yourself.

LAURA: I—I—never have had much
luck at—making friends.

(65) JIM: I don't see why you wouldn't.

LAURA: Well. I started out badly.

JIM: You mean being—

LAURA: Yes, it sort of—stood between
me—

(70) JIM: You shouldn't have let it!

LAURA: I know, but it did, and—

JIM: You were shy with people!

LAURA: I tried not to be but never
could—

(75) JIM: Overcome it?

LAURA: No, I—I never could!

JIM: I guess being shy is something
you have to work out of kind of
gradually.

(80) LAURA: [*sorrowfully*]. Yes—I guess it—

JIM: Takes time!

LAURA: Yes—

From *The Glass Menagerie* by Tennessee Williams.

16. Where did Laura and Jim first meet?
   (1) in school chorus
   (2) in a stairwell
   (3) in a hospital

17. Why did Laura always arrive late to
Chorus?
   (1) She didn't leave home in time.
   (2) She stayed too long talking to her
      friends.
   (3) She had a hard time getting
      upstairs.

18. When Laura says *To me it sounded
like—thunder!* (Line 34), she is talking
about the sound of
   (1) the chorus
   (2) her brace
   (3) other's laughter

19. Who first mentions the nickname Jim
gave Laura? _____

20. Which of the following conclusions
can you draw about Laura?
   (1) Although she was self-conscious
      in high school, she has recently
      become much more comfortable
      with herself.
   (2) She has changed from a sociable
      teenager into a withdrawn adult.
   (3) She has remained shy since
      childhood because of her handicap.

Questions 21 to 25 refer to the following
poem. Like many poems, this one is divided
into verses. In this case, there are six. The
verses are similar to paragraphs in that
each one has its own topic. Think about the
advice the poet gives.

ONE ART

The art of losing isn't hard to master;
so many things seem filled with the intent
to be lost that their loss is no disaster.

Lose something every day. Accept the fluster
(5) of lost door keys, the hour badly spent.
The art of losing isn't hard to master.

Then practice losing farther, losing faster:
places, and names, and where it was you meant
to travel. None of these will bring disaster.

(10) I lost my mother's watch. And look! my last, or
next-to-last, of three loved houses went.
The art of losing isn't hard to master.

I lost two cities, lovely ones. And, vaster,
some realms I owned, two rivers, a continent.
(15) I miss them, but it wasn't a disaster.

—Even losing you (the joking voice, a gesture
I love) I shan't have lied. It's evident
the art of losing's not too hard to master
though it may look like (*Write* it!) like disaster.

By Elizabeth Bishop.

21. What is the topic of the poem?
   (1) losing
   (2) favorite possessions
   (3) travel

22. In Lines 2–3, the words *so many things seem filled with the intent/to be lost* mean that some things
   (1) were never meant to be lost
   (2) are almost sure to be lost
   (3) can never be lost

23. The verse that begins *I lost two cities* (Lines 13–15) is about
   (1) war
   (2) natural disasters
   (3) moving away from familiar places

24. The word *vaster* in Line 13 means
   (1) smaller
   (2) larger
   (3) indeed

25. The poet would probably agree LEAST with which of the following?
   (1) Most of us think too much about possessions.
   (2) It is possible to overcome any loss.
   (3) Losing a loved one is as easy to handle as losing keys.

Questions 26 to 30 refer to the following passage about the opening of an exhibition of pictures by the artist Robert Rauschenberg. Rauschenberg is known for attaching unusual objects, such as a stuffed goat or a dirty quilt, to his paintings.

Some left the premises **precipitately**, others walked about looking dazed, and several brought their dismay to the attention of the artist, an extremely
(5) friendly, responsive, and clean-cut young Southerner of medium height and maximum charm, who made

earnest efforts to get to the bottom of their complaints.

(10)   One such conversation he remembers in detail. A middle-aged woman came up to him midway through the evening and asked why he was interested only in ugly things.

(15)   "She really wanted to know," Rauschenberg recalls. "You could see that she wasn't just being hostile. Well, I had to find out first of all what she meant by 'ugly,' and so we talked

(20)   about that for a while, and it seemed that what bothered her was the materials I'd chosen to use and the way they were put together. To her, all my decisions seemed absolutely

(25)   **arbitrary**—as though I could just as well have selected anything at all—and therefore there was no meaning, and that made it ugly. So I told her that if I were to describe the

(30)   way she was dressed, it might sound very much like what she'd been saying. For instance, she had feathers on her head. And she had this enamel brooch with a picture of **The Blue Boy**

(35)   on it pinned to her breast. And around her neck she had on what she would call mink but what could also be described as the skin of a dead animal. Well, at first she was a little offended

(40)   by this, I think, but then later she came back and said she was beginning to understand. She was really serious about it, and intelligent. The thing was, she just hadn't been able to *look*

(45)   at the pictures until somebody helped her."

From *The Bride and the Bachelors* by Calvin Tomkins.

---

precipitately: abruptly, suddenly
arbitrary: by chance, random
The Blue Boy: a famous painting from the 1700s

---

26. The words *Some left the premises precipitately* (Line 1) suggest that some people

   (1) left the exhibition in the rain
   (2) disliked what they saw
   (3) loved what they saw

27. The woman who talked to the artist was

   (1) hostile
   (2) stupid
   (3) puzzled

28. The artist discussed the meaning of what word with the middle-aged woman? _____

29. The artist told the middle-aged woman that

   (1) she was dressed badly
   (2) he could describe the way she was dressed and make it sound ugly
   (3) no matter what she said about his pictures, he thought she was dressed well

30. The artist seems to believe that

   (1) most people cannot understand modern art
   (2) people can learn, with help, to look at modern art
   (3) modern art has no meaning

Check your answers on page 180.

INTERPRETING LITERATURE AND THE ARTS READINGS 2
SKILLS CHART

To review the reading skills covered by the questions in Interpreting Literature and the Arts Readings 2, study the following parts of Units 1 and 2

Unit 1 Comprehending What You Read	Item Number
Chapter 1 Finding Details	1, 4, 8, 10, 11, 12, 13, 17, 22, 26, 28, 29
Chapter 2 Finding Topics and Main Ideas	6, 21, 23
Chapter 3 Reading Dialogue	19

Unit 2 Inferring As You Read	
Chapter 1 Inferring Unstated Details	2, 3, 7, 9, 14, 16, 18, 24, 27
Chapter 2 Inferring Ideas and Drawing Conclusions	5, 15, 20, 25, 30

INTERPRETING LITERATURE AND THE ARTS READINGS 2
CONTENT CHART

The following chart shows the type of reading passage each item in Interpreting Literature and the Arts Readings 2 refers to.

Type of Literature	Item Number
Nonfiction	6, 7, 8, 9, 10
Fiction	1, 2, 3, 4, 5, 11, 12, 13, 14, 15
Drama	16, 17, 18, 19, 20
Poetry	21, 22, 23, 24, 25
Commentary	26, 27, 28, 29, 30

GED PRACTICE 2

This section will give you more practice at answering questions like those on the GED. As you do this Practice, use the reading skills you've studied so far in this book.

Directions: Choose the <u>one best answer</u> to each item.

<u>Items 1 to 3</u> refer to the following passage.

HOW DOES THIS FAMILY REACT TO THE LOSS OF A JOB?

On the night my father came home from losing his job at the Wheatland Club, he told my mother about it straight out and they both acted as if it was a kind
(5) of joke. My mother did not get mad or seem upset or ask him why he had gotten fired. They both laughed about it. When we ate supper my mother sat at the table and seemed to be thinking. She said she
(10) could not get a job substituting until the term ended, but she would go to the school board and put her name in. She said other people would come to my father for work when it was known he
(15) was free, and that this was an opportunity in disguise—the reason we had come here—and that Montanans did not know gold when they saw it. She smiled at him when she said that. She
(20) said I could get a job, and I said I would. She said maybe she should become a banker, though she would need to finish college for that. And she laughed. Finally she said, 'You can do other things, Jerry.
(25) Maybe you've played enough golf for this lifetime.'

From "Electric City" by Richard Ford.

1. When the father lost his job, the narrator was probably
   (1) not yet born
   (2) an infant
   (3) a teenager
   (4) a young adult
   (5) an older adult

2. You can infer that the father was
   (1) a teacher
   (2) a banker
   (3) an office manager
   (4) a golfer
   (5) a farmer

3. Based on the passage, you can conclude that the mother
   (1) worries a lot—even about unimportant things
   (2) cannot accept change of any kind
   (3) adapts to new situations rather easily
   (4) looks at the negative side of things
   (5) tries to control other people

<u>Items 4 to 6</u> refer to the following paragraph.

WHEN DOES THIS OCTOGENARIAN FEEL BEST?

The new octogenarian feels as strong as ever when he is sitting back in a comfortable chair. He ruminates, he dreams, he remembers. He doesn't want
(5) to be disturbed by others. It seems to him that old age is only a costume assumed for those others; the true, the essential self is ageless. In a moment he will rise and go for a ramble in the woods, taking
(10) a gun along, or a fishing rod, if it is spring. Then he creaks to his feet, bending forward to keep his balance, and realizes that he will do nothing of the sort. The body and its surroundings have
(15) their messages for him or only one message: "You are old."

From <u>The View from 80</u> by Malcolm Cowley.

4. You can infer that an <u>octogenarian</u> (Line 1) is someone who is

   (1) strong
   (2) old
   (3) lonely
   (4) active
   (5) easily disturbed

5. According to the author, the new octogenarian feels fine when he is

   (1) relaxing in a chair
   (2) going for a walk
   (3) hunting
   (4) fishing
   (5) bending forward

6. The main idea of the paragraph is that when we are old,

   (1) our lives are a kind of illusion
   (2) both our bodies and our minds remind us of our age
   (3) our bodies seem to stay young, but our minds remind us of our age
   (4) our minds seem to stay young, but our bodies remind us of our age
   (5) we don't want to be disturbed

Items 7 to 10 are based on the following paragraph.

DOES GONZALO LIKE HIS JOB OR NOT?

I cannot think of anybody less suited to his vocation than Gonzalo. He dislikes the printed word, in the first place, and when he receives the mail he glares at it,
(5) letter by letter. The mail of foreigners sends him close to frenzy, and he so resents their confident expectation that <u>he</u> will take their mail to <u>them</u> that a small knot of the less trusting cluster
(10) around his door at mail time, stoking his irritability. Catch him at work in a garden and he is wryly amiable; but catch him in his cramped office or on his erratic round and he is a surly beast, an anti-mailman.
(15) Stories about him abound—mail in trees, old mail secreted in a trunk under his bed, his private hoard of postcards—but the villagers are mostly used to him and have found their own ways of prizing
(20) their mail loose from him. He has never delivered mail to me, for the house is the farthest outpost of inhabited land, and his bike could not climb to the ridge. But some years ago I took him a metal spring
(25) clip with my son's name, my own, and the name of the house pasted to it, and hung it on a nail in his office. He beamed with delight, as though I had invented the wheel, and has stuck our letters in it ever
(30) since. Even so, I occasionally receive a letter that is a year old. Where it has passed the interim, only Gonzalo knows.

From <u>Whereabouts</u> by Alastair Reid.

7. You can infer from the passage that Gonzalo is a

   (1) messenger
   (2) mailman
   (3) farmer
   (4) writer
   (5) fireman

8. Gonzalo never goes to the writer's house because

   (1) Gonzalo doesn't like the writer
   (2) Gonzalo refuses to go to foreigners' houses
   (3) the writer doesn't allow Gonzalo to visit
   (4) Gonzalo expects the writer to come to see him
   (5) Gonzalo's bike cannot make it up the hill

9. According to the passage, each of the following is or may be true about Gonzalo <u>except</u> that he

   (1) dislikes the printed word
   (2) puts mail in trees
   (3) keeps old mail in a trunk under his bed
   (4) burns packages
   (5) saves others' postcards

10. Which of the following titles best suits the paragraph?

   (1) How to Deal with a Difficult Person
   (2) The Spanish Postal Service
   (3) The Hardships of Being a Foreigner
   (4) A Man with the Wrong Job
   (5) The Mail Must Go Through

Check your answers on page 182.

GED PRACTICE 2 SKILLS CHART

To review the reading skills covered by the items in GED Practice 2, study the following parts of Units 1 and 2.

Unit 1 Comprehending What You Read	Item Number
Chapter 1 Finding Details	5, 8, 9
Chapter 2 Finding Topics and Main Ideas	10

Unit 2 Inferring As You Read	
Chapter 1 Inferring Unstated Details	1, 2, 4, 7
Chapter 2 Inferring Ideas and Drawing Conclusions	3, 6

GED PRACTICE 2 CONTENT CHART

The following chart shows the type of reading passage each item in GED Practice 2 refers to.

Type of Literature	Item Number
Nonfiction	4, 5, 6, 7, 8, 9, 10
Fiction	1, 2, 3

UNIT 3

Reading Critically

The first two units of this book concentrated on understanding what a writer has to say. This unit is about critical reading: applying, or using, what writers have to say and analyzing the ways they present their ideas.

In Chapter 1 of this unit you will learn to apply a writer's ideas to new situations. You will also learn to use what you find out about a character to imagine how he or she might act in a different situation. In Chapter 2 you will analyze passages of literature. You will learn how to discover what an author's purpose is in a particular passage. You will distinguish the facts from the opinions in a piece of writing. You will also learn how writers of fiction use characterization, setting, and mood. Finally, you will study some of the techniques writers use to create drama and poetry.

Novelist and short-story writer Flannery O'Connor. You will read three selections from her fiction in this unit.

Unit 3 Overview

Chapter 1   Applying What You Read
Chapter 2   Analyzing What You Read

_____

Interpreting Literature and the Arts Readings 3
GED Practice 3

1 APPLYING WHAT YOU READ

A measure of your understanding of a passage is your ability to use the writer's ideas in a different situation. If you can use a writer's ideas, you understand the writer's intentions well.

Lesson 12

Applying Ideas from Passages

In almost any passage you read, you will find out something about the writer's ideas. This is especially true with nonfiction. If you know how the writer thinks about one thing, you may be able to imagine how he or she would think about another. For example, if a writer expresses his or her ideas about education, you might be able to guess the writer's ideas about raising children.

To apply an author's ideas, you need to use your knowledge about ideas and human behavior. Think about what the author is saying in a passage. Try to figure out the author's attitudes and reactions. Then think about people you have met, or heard of, who believe or act as the author does.

TRY THIS

As you read the following paragraph, try to imagine the thoughts and feelings the writer had as the day he describes approached. Then answer the questions.

> I knew what would happen that day. In fact, in a way I was afraid it wouldn't. Nine hours and five minutes after I authorized removal of the respirator, my mother expired in a windowless private hospital room with the television on. We were both alone together then. She
> (5) was unconscious, I think. I was stroking her face and she was free of tubes at the end. I thought she would like that. I still do, most times. But some chilly nights, still long before dawn, I wonder in silence about the shadows of life and today's negotiated deaths.

From "The Ultimate Decision" by Andrew H. Malcolm.

What decision can you infer the writer made before the day described in the paragraph? _____

Does it seem that the writer found that decision easy to make or difficult to make? _____

How does the writer think his mother would have felt about his decision? _____

Before the day described in the paragraph, the writer must have decided to allow his mother to die rather than be kept alive by a respirator. The decision must have been difficult for him: the words *most times* in Line 6 suggest that he still sometimes wonders whether he made the right decision—the decision his mother would have wanted him to make. However, in Lines 5–6 he says he thought his mother *would like* being *free of tubes at the end.* That implies that the writer thinks his mother would have liked the decision.

Once you understand what the writer went through and how he felt about his decision, it is possible to imagine how the writer would act in another situation.

NOW TRY THIS

Apply your understanding of the writer by answering the following question.

If the writer had to decide whether or not to use life-sustaining equipment to keep his young wife alive, even though she would never come out of a coma, he would probably
  (1) keep her alive at all costs
  (2) allow her to die a natural death
  (3) be unable to make up his mind

If you apply what you know about the writer, you can assume that he would allow his wife to die—Choice (2). Her situation is similar enough to his mother's to let you guess that he would act as he had before. Of course, it is possible that the writer might make a different choice in this new situation, but it is reasonable to assume, based on what you know, that he would not.

Read the next three passages and answer the questions about each.

Some of the questions after each passage ask how well you understand what the writer means. Each passage also has one or more questions that ask you to apply something you understand from the passage to a new situation.

Questions 1 and 2 refer to the following passage. The author, Samuel Clemens, who lived from 1835 to 1910, used a pen name when he wrote: Mark Twain. His most famous books are *Tom Sawyer* and *The Adventures of Huckleberry Finn.*

Delegates at a political party convention.

Men think they think upon great political questions, and they do; but they think with their party, not independently; they read its literature but not that of the other side; they arrive at convictions but they are drawn from a partial view of the matter in hand and are of no

(5) particular value. They swarm with their party, they feel with their party, they are happy in their party's approval; and where the party leads they will follow, whether for right and honor or through blood and dirt and a mush of mutilated morals.

From "Corn-Pone Opinions" by Mark Twain.

1. The word *swarm* in Line 5 is usually used to describe the way some insects fly around in large groups. Mark Twain probably uses the word to emphasize his ideas that most people

    (1) think for themselves
    (2) don't think at all
    (3) think with the crowd

2. Mark Twain would probably expect a typical voter to

    (1) buy newspapers favoring different parties so that he could decide which candidates to vote for
    (2) vote for only the candidates backed by his party
    (3) listen carefully to debates so that he could decide which party to support.

Questions 3 to 7 refer to the following passage from an essay.

We teach our child many things I don't believe in, and almost nothing I do believe in. We teach punctuality, but I do not honestly think there is any considerable good in punctuality, particularly if the enforcement of it disturbs the peace. My father taught me, by example,

(5) that the greatest defeat in life was to miss a train. Only after many years did I learn that an escaping train carries away with it nothing vital to my health. Railroad trains are such magnificent objects we commonly mistake them for Destiny.

We teach cleanliness, sanitation, hygiene; but I am suspicious of

(10) these practices. A child who believes that every scratch needs to be painted with iodine has lost a certain grip on life that he may never regain and has acquired a **frailty** of spirit that may unfit him for living.

From "Sanitation" by E. B. White.

frailty: weakness

3. The word *punctuality* in both Lines 2 and 3 means
   (1) being on time
   (2) law enforcement
   (3) train schedules

4. The sentence *Only after many years did I learn that an escaping train carries away with it nothing vital to my health* (Lines 5–7) probably means that the author
   (1) has learned that it's okay to be late sometimes
   (2) knows now that trains are dangerous
   (3) worries about missing trains

5. If the author invited someone to lunch and that person arrived a half hour late, the author would probably
   (1) not mind very much
   (2) be very angry
   (3) feel defeated

6. If a child with a small cut on his leg came to the author, the author would most likely
   (1) drive the child to a hospital
   (2) tell the child to leave him alone
   (3) help the child to wash the cut and tell him to go back to play

7. The author would probably be most pleased if his child grew up to be someone who
   (1) gets to the airport at least an hour early
   (2) questions ideas that might not make sense
   (3) goes to bed at the first sign of a cold

Questions 8 to 10 refer to the following paragraph from another essay.

More and more, we take for granted that work must be **destitute of** pleasure. More and more, we assume that if we want to be pleased we must wait until evening, or the weekend, or vacation, or retirement. More and more, our farms and forests resemble our factories and

(5) offices, which in turn more and more resemble prisons—why else should we be so eager to escape them? We recognize defeated landscapes by the absence of pleasure from them. We are defeated at work because our work gives us no pleasure. . . . Where is our comfort but in the free, uninvolved, finally mysterious beauty and grace of this

(10) world that we did not make, that has no price? Where is our sanity but

there? Where is our pleasure but in working and resting kindly in the presence of this world?

From *What Are People For?: Essays* by Wendell Berry.

> *destitute of*: lacking

8. The author says in Line 5 that factories and offices *more and more resemble prisons* in order to point out that

    (1) modern architecture is bad
    (2) everything in America looks the same
    (3) people don't get much enjoyment from their work

9. To maintain good mental health, the author would probably advise someone to

    (1) get plenty of rest
    (2) find satisfying work
    (3) put money away for retirement

10. The author would probably most admire someone who

    (1) travels extensively
    (2) makes a living by pursuing a hobby
    (3) spends a lot of free time in the woods

Check your answers on page 182.

Lesson 13

Applying Knowledge about Characters

Usually when you read fiction, you find out a lot about the various characters in a story or novel. Knowing how a certain character acts in one situation can help you guess how that character might act in another situation. For example, if a writer describes a character who loses his temper quickly, you might be able to imagine how that character would act under stress.

As you read about a character, try to figure out the character's attitudes. Imagine how that character would act in situations other than the ones the author describes.

TRY THIS

As you read the following passage from a short story by a Canadian writer, think about the differences between the characters in the two families. Then answer the questions.

Dr. Peebles was staying at our place for dinner, having just helped one of our cows have twins, and he said I looked smart to him and his wife was looking for a girl to help. He said she felt tied down, with the two children, out in the country. I guess she would,
(5) my mother said, being polite, though I could tell from her face she was wondering what on earth it would be like to have only two children and no barn work, and then to be complaining.

When I went home I would describe to them the work I had to do, and it made everybody laugh. Mrs. Peebles had an automatic
(10) washer and dryer, the first I ever saw. I have had those in my own home for such a long time now it's hard to remember how much of a miracle it was to me, not having to struggle with the wringer and hang up and haul down. Let alone not having to heat water. Then there was practically no baking. Mrs. Peebles said she couldn't
(15) make pie crust, the most amazing thing I ever heard a woman admit. I could, of course, and I could make light biscuits and a white cake and a dark cake, but they didn't want it, she said they watched their figures.

From "How I Met My Husband" by Alice Munro.

When the girl went home and described her work, everybody laughed (Lines 8–9). This shows the family's

  (1) pleasure in the way the girl tells a story
  (2) contempt for the Peebles family
  (3) amazement at the light work at the Peebles' house

If, one day, the girl and her mother learned that they had to prepare a dinner for fifteen farm workers, they would probably

  (1) protest that they needed more time
  (2) start cooking
  (3) refuse

The laughter indicates amazement at the light work at the doctor's house—Choice 3. In Lines 6–7 the girl's mother wondered *what on earth it would be like to have only two children and no barn work.* The girl and her family are clearly accustomed to hard work. Another clue to this is that the Peebles' automatic washer and dryer was the first the girl ever saw (Lines 9–10). Nothing indicates that the girl is an especially good storyteller, and there is no evidence of contempt for the Peebles family.

Since the girl and her mother are accustomed to hard work, they would probably start cooking, Choice (2).

Read the next three passages and answer the questions about each. Some of the questions after each passage ask how well you understand how the characters react to certain things. Each passage also has one or more questions that ask you to imagine how one of the characters would act in a new situation.

Questions 1 to 3 refer to the following passage from a short story. Think about the narrator's reactions to his travels.

When I crossed Minnesota, I found—in fact I saw it myself, firsthand—that there were as many Swedes as Germans there. And funny names—say, they certainly had the funniest names! Swanson and Kettleson and Shipstead, and all like that—simply screams. I says
(5) to Mama, ''Well, Mrs. Schmaltz,'' I says—I often call her that when we're funning around—''Well, Mrs. Schmaltz,'' I says, ''you wanted to get a kick out of this trip, and here you got it,'' I says, ''in all these funny names.''
And all like that.
(10) We get to thinking, here in Zenith, that everybody, I mean every *normal* fellow, lives just like we do, but out there in Minnesota I found a lot of the folks never even heard of our mayor here in Zenith—they just talked about Minneapolis and Saint Paul politics! I tell you, travel like that gives a fellow a whole new set of insights into human
(15) character and how big the world is, after all, and as our pastor, Dr. Edwards, often says, the capacity of the Lord for producing new sets of psychological setups is practically, you might say, absolutely unlimited.

From ''Travel Is So Broadening'' by Sinclair Lewis.

1. The names the narrator encountered on his trip are funny to him because
   (1) Minnesota is known for its unusual names
   (2) the narrator cannot speak English well
   (3) the names are not like the ones the character is familiar with

2. The narrator's surprise that many people in Minnesota never heard of the mayor of Zenith indicates the narrator's

   (1) hatred of strangers
   (2) vast travel experience
   (3) small-town outlook

3. If the narrator were offered unfamiliar foreign food, he would probably

   (1) refuse to eat it
   (2) talk about its strangeness
   (3) throw it away

Questions 4 to 6 refer to the following paragraph from another short story. Think about what General Sash likes.

General Sash was a hundred and four years old. He lived with his granddaughter, Sally Poker Sash, who was sixty-two years old and who prayed every night on her knees that he would live until her graduation from college. The General didn't give two slaps for her graduation but
(5) he never doubted he would live for it. Living had got to be such a habit with him that he couldn't conceive of any other condition. A graduation exercise was not exactly his idea of a good time, even if, as she said, he would be expected to sit on the stage in his uniform. She said there would be a long procession of teachers and students in their robes but
(10) that there wouldn't be anything to equal *him* in his uniform. He knew this well enough without her telling him, and as for the damn procession, it could march to hell and back and not cause him a quiver. He liked parades with floats full of Miss Americas and Miss Daytona Beaches and Miss Queen Cotton Products. He didn't have any use for
(15) processions and a procession full of schoolteachers was about as deadly as **the River Styx** to his way of thinking. However, he was willing to sit on the stage in his uniform so that they could see him.

From "A Late Encounter with the Enemy" by Flannery O'Connor.

> *the River Styx:* in Greek mythology, the river across which the spirits of the dead were carried

4. The reaction General Sash has in Lines 4–5 to the graduation plans indicates his

   (1) respect for education
   (2) love for his granddaughter
   (3) confidence that he will live on and on

5. The statement *He knew this well enough without her telling him* (Lines 10–11) indicates General Sash's

   (1) pride
   (2) good memory
   (3) age

6. Which of the following would be most likely to amuse General Sash?

   (1) an open house in honor of the general himself
   (2) an award ceremony for his granddaughter
   (3) a party to honor the Teacher of the Year

Questions 7 to 11 refer to the following passage by a writer who shares a love of fishing with his friend, Deeds.

Deeds is a gentle, ordinarily taciturn soul of forty-two who occupies a ramshackle cottage on a thirty-acre prune ranch. He has as little tolerance for **pretense** as anybody I've ever known. Once, on his birthday, I gave him a reprint edition of Zane Grey's classic *Tales of*
(5) *Fresh-Water Fishing*, which contains a marvelously **florid** story, "Rocky Riffle," about fishing for steelhead on the Rogue River, in Oregon. The book was a risky gift, because of its **pervasive** floridness, and also because Deeds is not much of a reader—he sticks to the evening paper and supermarket scandal sheets. He thanked me for the
(10) book, then leafed through it and looked at the pictures, stopping when he came to one that showed Grey, in a flat-brimmed hat, **cavorting** on a snowy hillside with three bears. The photograph was captioned, THE BEARS ON THE WAY TO CRATER LAKE—TAME BUT NOT VERY!

"What's this got to do with steelhead?" Deeds asked.
(15) I explained that Grey, like Jack London or Ernest Hemingway, was a larger-than-life character.

"You can't be larger than life," said Deeds. "That's a contradiction in terms. Here, listen to this stuff. 'The steelhead lay flat on the gravel. I stared, longing for the art of the painter, so as to **perpetuate** the
(20) exquisite hues and contours of that fish. All trout are beautiful. But this one of sea species seemed more than beautiful. He gaped, he quivered.'"

"You've got to take it with a grain of salt, Paul," I said. "It's from another era."

From "Steelhead on the Russian" by Bill Barich.

pretense: a false show of something
florid: overly flowery in style
pervasive: spread throughout
cavorting: jumping around happily
perpetuate: keep alive forever

7. Because Deeds has *little tolerance for pretense* (Line 3), he would probably feel most comfortable with someone who

    (1) pretends to be something he isn't

    (2) tries to impress people by a flashy style

    (3) is "just folks"

8. Which of the following is a reason why the book was a risky gift?

    (1) Deeds didn't like Zane Grey.

    (2) Reading wasn't a big interest of Deeds'.

    (3) The book had too many pictures.

9. When Deeds says *Here, listen to this stuff* (Line 18) about Zane Grey's flowery writing, he shows that he

    (1) likes it

    (2) doesn't understand it

    (3) doesn't like it

10. Which of the following would Deeds be most likely to do for amusement?

    (1) discuss novels with fellow members of a reading club

    (2) stay at home and read a newspaper

    (3) take a drive in a new sportscar

11. Deeds probably never wears

    (1) a work shirt

    (2) a tuxedo

    (3) jeans

Check your answers on page 183.

Chapter

2 ANALYZING WHAT YOU READ

When you analyze something, you look at it very closely. In a sense, you pick it apart to see how it's made or how it works. As you will learn in this chapter, passages from literature, like almost anything else, can be analyzed. You can look at their parts and see how they have the effect they do.

Lesson 14

The Author's Purpose (Nonfiction)

In Lesson 10 you learned that some passages—especially ones from fiction—don't have clear main ideas. Rather, many such passages have a main purpose: to tell or show something about a character or an event. This lesson looks even more closely at authors' purposes in writing.

Whenever a writer writes, he or she has a purpose. To tell or to show something is the purpose of a lot of writing, but writers write with other purposes, too. The various kinds of articles in a newspaper illustrate some of the purposes writers can have. The journalists who report news write to inform. They give readers details about events. The editors who write for the "editorial" or opinion page often try to persuade. For example, they may try to convince a reader to support certain issues or to vote for certain candidates. Sports writers often have at least two purposes. As they describe a game, they inform, but with their descriptions, they also hope to entertain readers.

To understand a writer's purpose in a passage, first find the topic of the passage. Sometimes it helps to note the main idea, too. Then, watch for words that show the attitude of the writer. Is the writer positive or negative toward his or her subject? Ask yourself whether the writer wants to inform you about something, to express an opinion about something, or to convince you of something. Also ask yourself whether the writer is trying to entertain you with his or her choice of words.

Read the next paragraph and answer the questions that follow it.

Vigorous writing is **concise.** A sentence should contain no unnecessary words, a paragraph no unnecessary sentences, for the same reason that a drawing should have no unnecessary lines and a machine no unnecessary parts. This requires not that the writer
(5) make all his sentences short, or that he avoid all detail and treat his subjects only in outline, but that every word tell.

From *The Elements of Style* by William Strunk, Jr., and E. B. White.

---

vigorous: strong, forceful
concise: free from extra detail

The paragraph is about
(1) drawing
(2) writing
(3) machinery

Of the following, the best statement of the main idea of the paragraph is that
(1) forceful writing does not contain unnecessary words or sentences
(2) writing can be compared to drawing or machinery
(3) words are used to tell

Which of the following best describes the authors' purpose?
(1) to give their opinion about what makes good writing
(2) to amuse the reader with unusual comparisons
(3) to convince the reader to learn to write forcefully

The topic of the paragraph is writing, Choice (2). The main idea is that forceful writing contains no unnecessary words or sentences, Choice (1). The authors' purpose in writing the paragraph is to give an opinion, Choice (1), which is just what they do in the main idea. They use unusual comparisons more to help explain their opinion than to amuse. They don't try to convince the reader to learn to write forcefully. If that had been their purpose, they probably would have contrasted the advantages of writing well to the disadvantages of writing poorly.

Read the following passages and answer the questions about them. The questions will help you discover the author's purpose in writing each passage.

Questions 1 to 4 refer to the following paragraph from a book about travel. The author talks, in part, about Venice, the Italian city famous for its canals.

Over the hundreds of years that visitors from abroad have been attracted to Venice, they must have responded to its charms in a great variety of ways, but it's probably not common to hear them say, "You know, it reminds me a bit of Kansas City." The reason I was an
(5) exception goes back to my **infatuation** with markets. I am a sucker for not just the weekly market in the square of a small French town but the wholesale city market that caters to people like produce distributors and restaurant **proprietors**. The section of the Venice market I was strolling through was like that, except that the characteristic
(10) city-market sound of trucks in low gear was missing. . . . In New York, I'm a regular at the Saturday market in Union Square, where farmers come from upstate and New Jersey and Pennsylvania to sell fruits and vegetables to miraculously cheerful New Yorkers; when the **legendary** baker from Yonkers arrives at her usual spot, rather late in the
(15) morning as market time goes, I stand patiently with the other **devotees** as she and her husband unload a car that contains a steaming tray of something too good to be called cheesecake. I like the couple from Yonkers—I like market people and the market atmosphere in general—but I'd stand in line to buy that cheesecake from someone who
(20) had the personality of my old Latin teacher.

From "Full Italian Basket" by Calvin Trillin.

> **infatuation:** love, admiration
> **proprietors:** owners
> **legendary:** well-known
> **devotees:** people who are devoted,
>   loyal, and faithful to an idea or a person

1. What is the topic of the paragraph?

   (1) Venice
   (2) food
   (3) markets
   (4) Kansas City

2. According to the author, how was the Venice market different from markets in other cities?

   (1) There were more foreigners in the Venice market.
   (2) There was no sound of trucks in the Venice market.
   (3) The customers in the Venice market were all restaurant owners.

3. From the last sentence in the passage, you can infer that the author's Latin teacher was

   (1) a warm and loveable soul
   (2) a part-time market worker
   (3) a difficult person

4. The author's main purpose in writing this paragraph was to

   (1) explain the difference between markets in Venice and New York
   (2) amuse readers while expressing his enjoyment of markets
   (3) convince readers that it's better to shop in markets than in stores

Questions 5 to 9 refer to the following passage about a now torn-down baseball park.

The things I liked best about the Polo Grounds were sights and emotions so inconsequential that they will surely slide out of my recollection. A flight of pigeons flashing out of the barn-shadow of the upper stands, wheeling past the right-field foul pole, and disappearing
(5) above the **inert,** heat-heavy flags on the roof. The steepness of the ramp descending from the Speedway toward the upper-stand gates, which pushed your toes into your shoe tips as you approached the park, tasting sweet anticipation and getting out your change to buy a program. The unmistakable, final "*Plock!*" of a line drive hitting the
(10) green wooden barrier above the stands in deep left field. The gentle, rockerlike swing of the loop of rusty chain you rested your arm upon in a box seat, and the heat of the sun-warmed iron coming through your shirtsleeve under your elbow. At a night game, the moon rising out of the scoreboard like a spongy, day-old orange balloon and then

(15) **whitening over the waves of noise and the slow, shifting clouds of floodlit cigarette smoke. All these I mourn, for their loss constitutes the death of still another neighborhood—a small landscape of distinctive and reassuring familiarity.**

From *The Summer Game* by Roger Angell.

> *inert:* not moving

5. The topic of the passage is

   (1) baseball
   (2) the Polo Grounds
   (3) ball parks

6. When the writer describes the things he liked as *inconsequential* (Line 2), he probably means that they were

   (1) powerful
   (2) unusual
   (3) unimportant

7. The word *plock* in Line 9 is probably supposed to

   (1) suggest the sound of a ball hitting a wooden wall
   (2) name a certain play in baseball
   (3) be a word the umpire says

8. Which of the following best describes the author's feelings now that the Polo Grounds have been torn down?

   (1) He is glad that the neighborhood will be improved.
   (2) He misses the place.
   (3) He doesn't want to stand in the way of progress.

9. Which of the following was probably NOT one of the author's reasons for writing the piece?

   (1) to convince the reader that old ball parks were better than new ones
   (2) to write a word picture of the ball park
   (3) to share his memories of the ball park
   (4) to entertain the reader with his descriptions

Questions 10 to 13 refer to the following passage from a speech by a famous historian.

The commonest question asked of historians by **laymen** is whether history serves a purpose. Is it useful? Can we learn from the lessons of history?

(5) When people want history to be **utilitarian** and teach us lessons, that means they also want to be sure that it meets scientific standards. This, in my opinion, it cannot do, for reasons which I will come to in a moment. To practice history as a science is sociology, an altogether different discipline which I personally find **antipathetic**—although I suppose the sociologists would consider that my **deficiency** rather

(10) than theirs. The sociologists plod along with their noses to the ground assembling masses of statistics in order to arrive at some obvious conclusion which a reasonably **perceptive** historian, not to mention a large part of the general public, knows anyway, simply from observation—that social mobility is increasing, for instance, or that

(15) women have different problems from men. One wishes they would just cut loose someday, lift up their heads, and look at the world around them.

If history were a science, we should be able to get a grip on her, learn her ways, establish her patterns, know what will happen

(20) tomorrow. Why is it that we cannot? The answer lies in what I call the Unknowable **Variable**—namely, man. Human beings are always and finally the subject of history. History is the record of human behavior, the most fascinating subject of all, but illogical and so crammed with an unlimited number of variables that it is not **susceptible of** the

(25) scientific method nor of systematizing.

From "Is History a Guide to the Future?" by Barbara Tuchman.

> **laymen:** non-professionals, people who are not experts
> **utilitarian:** useful
> **antipathetic:** not likeable, distasteful
> **deficiency:** lack of something
> **perceptive:** able to grasp mentally
> **variable:** something that is changeable, unpredictable
> **susceptible of:** affected by

10. What is the topic of this passage?

    (1) sociology
    (2) history
    (3) statistics

11. According to the author, the subject of history is

    (1) events and dates
    (2) the scientific method
    (3) human beings
    (4) sociology

12. The author thinks that history is *illogical* (Line 23) because

    (1) it is not a science
    (2) sociologists go about things the wrong way
    (3) human beings are unpredictable

13. The author's purpose is to

    (1) explain why history cannot meet scientific standards
    (2) convince the reader that history is more important than science
    (3) entertain the reader with stories about history

Check your answers on page 184.

Lesson 15

Facts and Opinions
(Commentary on the Arts)

A convincing writer may make readers think that every word he or she writes is the truth. But much of what writers have to say expresses their opinions. One food writer praises cabbage. Another goes on about how awful cabbage is.

To separate facts from opinions, ask yourself whether each statement in a piece of writing can be proved or not. If a drama critic says that an actor forgot his lines several times during a performance, you can prove that by talking to witnesses—other people who saw the same performance. If they also noticed that the actor forgot his lines, you can accept it for fact. If the writer of a biography tells you that the subject was born in 1921, you know that this can probably be proved. A birth certificate or hospital records can confirm the writer's statement. You can accept the date of birth as fact.

If the writer says that the subject was a good, selfless, generous person, you may believe the writer. Remember, however, that this is opinion. It may even be the opinion of many people, but it is not the sort of thing that can be proved easily.

Commentary on the arts is writing that is full of both fact and opinion. For example, a drama critic owes it to his or her readers to give them an idea of what a performance was like and what the play itself was like. While reporting facts about both these things, the critic is sure to give opinions about the quality of the performance and of the play. Sometimes within just one sentence a writer will include both a fact and an opinion.

TRY THIS

The following passage is from a weekly magazine noted for high-quality writing. The review is unusual, in part, because it describes an amateur, or nonprofessional, performance. As you read the passage, try to distinguish between the facts and the opinions the author includes. Then answer the question that follows the passage.

"Oklahoma!" opened on March 31, 1943, and they say that when it did, musical-theatre history was made. But we don't think the excitement of that occasion can compare with the excitement we felt, the other night, when Robbie Horwitz came down the aisle of the
(5) auditorium at P.S. 41 singing, "There's a bright golden haze on the meadow . . . ," and took up a stance on the stage steps. We don't actually know Robbie Horwitz (or anyone else connected with the show; we were there because a friend had said he was going off to a sixth-grade production of "Oklahoma!" and we'd said, Not without us
(10) you're not). But something about the way the kid sang—without polish or prissiness, going after the high notes the way he'd go after a fastball, say—won our heart.
For us, Rayme Sciaroni's production represented some sort of **pinnacle.** It was partly the three cows painted on a backdrop in
(15) different perspectives (we took a particular shine to the cow that was looking at the audience head-on) and partly the way the kids sang. It was partly the way the production (and everyone in it managed to be topnotch without being **precocious.** Through all the cries of "Shhh!" and "Quiet, please!" from audience members with little sympathy for
(20) certain people's smaller brothers and sisters, there was no **smirking** or knowingness, just an openhearted embracing of the material.

Excerpted from *The New Yorker*.

> *pinnacle:* high point, peak
> *precocious:* mature at an unusually early age
> *smirking:* smiling in a self-satisfied way

The following statements come from the passage. Some of them repeat just part of a sentence in the passage. Tell whether each statement is a fact or an opinion.

_____ "Oklahoma!" opened on March 31, 1943. (Line 1)

_____ We don't think the excitement of that occasion can compare with the excitement we felt, the other night. (Lines 2–4)

_____ Robbie Horwitz came down the aisle of the auditorium at P.S. 41. (Lines 4–5)

_____ We don't actually know Robbie Horwitz. (Lines 6–7)

_____ For us, Rayme Sciaroni's production represented some sort of pinnacle. (Lines 13–14)

_____ The production (and everyone in it) managed to be topnotch. (Lines 17–18)

The second and last two statements are opinions. The first three words of the second statement announce that it is an opinion. It begins *we don't think.* When someone says, "I think" or "I don't think," what follows is usually an opinion. In the next-to-last statement, the words *For us* work the same way. They mean "in our opinion." The last statement is about the quality of the performance, which is necessarily an opinion. Other people who saw the same performance might not have thought it was topnotch.

The first, third, and fourth statements are facts. By looking at records, it would be possible to prove when "Oklahoma!" opened. By talking to witnesses, it would be possible to prove that Robbie Horwitz came down the aisle and that the writer does not know him personally.

The difference between statements of fact and statements of opinion is that facts can be proved, but opinions cannot. Remember this difference as you do the following exercise.

EXERCISE 15

Read the next two passages and answer the questions about each. Some of the questions ask about your comprehension of the passage. Most of the questions ask you to analyze statements the writer makes and to decide whether they are facts or opinions.

Questions 1 to 4 refer to the following passage taken from a movie review. Like the review of "Oklahoma!," it comes from *The New Yorker* magazine. Try to picture the scene the reviewer describes.

In the middle of "My Left Foot," the movie about the **Dubliner** Christy Brown, a victim of cerebral palsy who became a painter and a writer, Christy (Daniel Day-Lewis) is in a restaurant, at a dinner party celebrating the opening of an exhibition of the pictures he painted by
(5) holding a brush between his toes. For some time, he has been misinterpreting the friendly manner of the woman doctor who has been training him, and who arranged the show, and now, high on booze and success, he erupts. "I love you, Eileen," he says, and then, sharing his happiness with the others at the table, "I love you all." Eileen, not
(10) comprehending that his love for her is passionate and sexual, takes the occasion to announce that she's going to marry the gallery owner in six months. In his **staccato**, distorted speech, Christy spits out "Con-grat-u-la-tions" so that the syllables sound like slaps, and he lashes her with "I'm glad you taught me to speak so I could say that,
(15) Eileen." The restaurant is suddenly quiet: everyone is watching his torment as he beats his head on the table and yanks the tablecloth off with his teeth.

It's all very fast, and it may be the most emotionally wrenching scene I've ever experienced at the movies. There's nothing soft or
(20) **maudlin** about this movie's view of Christy.

From *The New Yorker*, October 2, 1989, by Pauline Kael.

> ***Dubliner:*** a person from Dublin, Ireland
> ***staccato:*** abrupt, disconnected
> ***maudlin:*** overly sentimental

1. In Lines 1–2, the reviewer says that "My Left Foot" is a *movie about the Dubliner Christy Brown*. Can you accept this statement as a fact, or is it an opinion? _____

2. The reviewer describes a scene that takes place in

   (1) a restaurant
   (2) an art gallery
   (3) a bar in Dublin

3. What is unusual about the way Christy Brown paints? _____

4. Which of the following statements from the review expresses a fact?
   (1) Christy spits out "Con-grat-u-la-tions." (Lines 12–13)
   (2) It's all very fast. (Line 18)
   (3) There's nothing soft or maudlin about this movie's view of Christy. (Lines 19–20)

Questions 5 to 12 refer to the following passage from a book review. The subject of the review is unusual.

Owner's manuals have a long and tradition-filled history. It is not a tradition that has brought much joy to the hearts of automobile owners, however. Such manuals have never been easy to read—not once, since they first appeared in the 19th century. They **eschew** all
(5) literary devices whatsoever, such as plot, characterization, humor, suspense, imagery and point of view. They include instructions written in a prose so dense as to make them of little or no use in actually operating the machine they are intended to accompany.

Even worse, most owner's manuals contain a great deal of surplus
(10) information. Companies that gladly spend hundreds of thousands of dollars on a machine will try to save a dollar or two on the manual by writing it to serve several other machines at the same time; for two, three, even four models, one manual. One for two types of Kenmore freezer, three sizes of John Deere tractor, four kinds of Hardwick
(15) kitchen stove. The unhappy purchaser is thus confronted with what amounts to a guessing game. In the Hardwick stove manual, for example, you learn this: "Your appliance is equipped with either an **EFFLEX** or a **TRI-TEMP** surface burner valve. The valve can be identified by the markings on the control knob." Wonderful! . . .
(20) "1990 Chevrolet S-10 Owner's Manual" mostly upholds the old tradition. Its confusingly numbered pages (typical page number:2D-6) attempt to cover not one but three different Chevrolet models: the Blazer and two varieties of light truck. This makes for difficulties. Suppose you get a flat tire in your Blazer or your regular pickup or your
(25) extended-cab pickup. In each the jack is stored in a different place, so that it can require a thorough study of pages 3–9 through 3–12 just to find out where to look for it (and how to extract it when found). By a piece of inspired bad planning, these four pages of instructions for finding your jack come after the directions for changing a tire. The
(30) owner, already **sullen** because of the flat, may be tempted to hurl the jack, when it finally is found, through the optional sliding rear window.

From "Getting to Know Your Synchronized Input Shaft," by Noel Perrin.

eschew: avoid
sullen: depressed and gloomy

5. What is the subject of the book review?

   (1) novels about cars
   (2) owner's manuals
   (3) writing

6. In Line 4, the author says that owner's manuals *first appeared in the 19th century.* Is his statement a fact or an opinion? _____

7. In Lines 6–7, the author says that manuals for automobile owners are *written in a prose so dense as to make them of little or no use.* Is this statement fact or an opinion? _____

8. According to Lines 17–18, the manual for Hardwick stoves says, *"Your appliance is equipped with either an EFFLEX or a TRI-TEMP surface burner valve."* Can you take it for a fact that the manual says that, or is it an opinion? _____

9. The author's opinion of the *1990 Chevrolet S-10 Owner's Manual* (Line 20) is that it is

   (1) a great improvement over the typical manual
   (2) as bad as most owner's manuals
   (3) probably the most clearly written of all manuals

10. In Line 21, the author says that a certain Chevrolet owner's manual has pages that are *confusingly numbered.* Is his statement about the page numbering a fact or an opinion? _____

11. In Lines 28–29, the author says that in the Chevrolet owner's manual, the *instructions for finding your jack come after the directions for changing a tire.* Is what the author says about the instructions for finding a jack a fact or an opinion? _____

12. Overall, the author's opinion about owner's manuals seems to be that they are

    (1) easy to use
    (2) frustrating to use
    (3) impossible to use

Check your answers on page 184.

Characterization (Fiction)

Fiction, usually in the form of novels or short stories, has human beings and their relationships as its principal topic. One of the purposes of fiction is to teach us about ourselves.

Characterization means representing human beings with words. As soon as an author introduces a character, begin to collect in your mind the writer's descriptions of that character. Pay careful attention to the words that describe the character. Decide what kind of person you think he or she is. Start to guess what the character might do.

Sometimes, instead of simply telling you what a character is like, writers use **anecdotes,** short descriptions of some event, to develop characterization. In these short descriptions you learn how characters react to certain situations. You learn something about their nature.

TRY THIS

The character described in the next passage is one of the two main characters in a novel. The other character, by the way, is his twin brother. Read the passage and answer the questions that follow.

Lewis was tall and stringy, with shoulders set square and a steady long-limbed stride. Even at eighty he could walk over the hills all day, or wield an axe all day, and not get tired.

He gave off a strong smell. His eyes—grey, dreamy and
(5) **astygmatic**—were set well back into the skull, and capped with thick round lenses in white metal frames. He bore the scar of a cycling accident on his nose and, ever since, its tip had curved downwards and turned purple in cold weather.

His head would wobble as he spoke: unless he was fumbling
(10) with his watch-chain, he had no idea what to do with his hands. In company he always wore a puzzled look; and if anyone made a statement of fact, he'd say, "Thank you!" or "Very kind of you!" Everyone agreed he had a wonderful way with sheepdogs.

From *On the Black Hill* by Bruce Chatwin.

astygmatic: having blurred vision

According to Lines 1–3, Lewis seems to be
(1) frail
(2) strong
(3) confused

The statement *in company he always wore a puzzled look*
(Lines 10–11) probably means that Lewis
(1) couldn't hear
(2) was uncomfortable
(3) didn't understand the things people said to him

Which of the following did Lewis probably enjoy doing LEAST?
(1) taking a walk through the hills
(2) tending to the sheepdogs
(3) gossiping with local farmers
(4) chopping wood

Many words in Lines 1–3 suggest that Lewis is strong—
Choice (2): He is *stringy, with shoulders set square* and a *long-limbed stride. He could walk over the hills* or *wield an axe all day, and not get tired.*

His puzzled look probably means that he was uncomfortable—
Choice (2). Around people, he didn't know what to do with his hands, and he didn't say appropriate things.

Lewis would probably least like gossiping with local farmers—
Choice (3)—since he was uncomfortable with people. He seemed to prefer physical activity: walking (Line 2), wielding an axe (Line 3), cycling (Line 6), tending sheepdogs (Line 13).

EXERCISE 16

Read the next three passages and answer the questions about the characters in each.

Questions 1 to 5 refer to the following passage. They are the first two paragraphs from a short story. Think about what the grandmother is trying to do.

The grandmother didn't want to go to Florida. She wanted to visit some of her connections in east Tennessee and she was seizing at every chance to change Bailey's mind. Bailey was the son she lived with, her only boy. He was sitting on the edge of his chair at the table, bent over
(5) the orange sports section of the *Journal.* "Now look here, Bailey," she said, "see here, read this," and she stood with one hand on her thin hip

and the other rattling the newspaper at his bald head. "Here this fellow that calls himself The Misfit is aloose from the Federal Pen and headed toward Florida and you read here what it says he did to these people. Just you read it. I wouldn't take my children in any direction with a criminal like that aloose in it. I couldn't answer to my conscience if I did."

Bailey didn't look up from his reading so she wheeled around then and faced the children's mother, a young woman in slacks, whose face was as broad and innocent as a cabbage and was tied around with a green head-kerchief that had two points on the top like rabbit's ears. She was sitting on the sofa, feeding the baby his apricots out of a jar. "The children have been to Florida before," the old lady said. "You all ought to take them somewhere else for a change so they would see different parts of the world and be broad. They never have been to east Tennessee."

From "A Good Man Is Hard to Find" by Flannery O'Connor.

1. Where did the grandmother want to go?

    (1) Georgia
    (2) Florida
    (3) Tennessee

2. Bailey is the grandmother's

    (1) husband
    (2) son
    (3) grandson

3. The young woman wearing a green head-kerchief is probably

    (1) Bailey's daughter
    (2) Bailey's wife
    (3) the grandmother's sister

4. When the grandmother says *I wouldn't take my children in any direction with a criminal like that aloose in it* (Lines 10–11), she is probably trying

    (1) to make Bailey a better father
    (2) to protect her family
    (3) to persuade Bailey to go where she wants

5. The grandmother *was seizing at every chance to change Bailey's mind* (Lines 2–3), because she

    (1) thought Bailey had formed a wrong opinion about something
    (2) was determined to get her way
    (3) was concerned about her grandchildren

Questions 6 to 10 refer to the following paragraph from a novel. Think about the way Macon's daughters react to him.

Solid, rumbling, likely to erupt without prior notice, Macon kept each member of his family awkward with fear. His hatred of his wife glittered and sparked in every word he spoke to her. The disappointment he felt in his daughters sifted down on them like ash, (5) dulling their buttery complexions and choking the lilt out of what should have been girlish voices. Under the frozen heat of his glance they tripped over doorsills and dropped the salt cellar into the yolks of their poached eggs. The way he mangled their grace, wit, and self-esteem was the single excitement of their days. Without the (10) tension and drama he ignited, they might not have known what to do with themselves.

From *Song of Solomon* by Toni Morrison.

6. What word does the author use to describe Macon's feelings toward his wife?

   (1) hatred
   (2) love
   (3) disappointment

7. What word does the author use to describe Macon's feeling toward his daughters?

   (1) hatred
   (2) love
   (3) disappointment

8. Why do the daughters trip and drop things?

   (1) Their fear of their father makes them awkward.
   (2) They are naturally clumsy.
   (3) They are very small.

9. The last sentence in the paragraph implies that the daughters

   (1) didn't pay any attention to their father
   (2) were emotionally controlled by the way their father treated them
   (3) depended on their father to tell them what to do each day

10. From the paragraph you can infer that Macon is a man

   (1) with a strong temper who makes harsh judgments
   (2) who is warm and supportive
   (3) with a quick sense of humor

Questions 11 to 15 refer to the following passage, which introduces the main character in a novel.

A green hunting cap squeezed the top of the fleshy balloon of a head. The green earflaps, full of large ears and uncut hair and the fine bristles that grew in the ears themselves, stuck out on either side like turn signals indicating two directions at once. Full, pursed lips
(5)   protruded beneath the bushy black moustache and, at their corners, sank into little folds filled with disapproval and potato chip crumbs. In the shadow under the green visor of the cap Ignatius J. Reilly's **supercilious** blue and yellow eyes looked down upon the other people waiting under the clock at the D. H. Holmes department store, studying
(10) the crowd of people for signs of bad taste in dress. Several of the outfits, Ignatius noticed, were new enough and expensive enough to be properly considered offenses against taste and decency. Possession of anything new or expensive only reflected a person's lack of theology and geometry; it could even cast doubts upon one's soul.
(15)   Ignatius himself was dressed comfortably and sensibly. The hunting cap prevented head colds. The voluminous tweed trousers were durable and permitted unusually free locomotion. Their pleats and nooks contained pockets of warm, stale air that soothed Ignatius. The plaid flannel shirt made a jacket unnecessary while the muffler
(20) guarded exposed Reilly skin between earflap and collar. The outfit was acceptable by any theological and geometrical standards, however **abstruse**, and suggested a rich inner life.

From *A Confederacy of Dunces* by John Kennedy Toole.

> *supercilious:* having an air of superiority
> *abstruse:* difficult to comprehend

11. In a crowd Ignatius J. Reilly watched how people
    (1) dressed
    (2) behaved
    (3) talked

12. Reilly's appearance could be described as
    (1) strange
    (2) ordinary
    (3) attractive

13. Reilly considered clothes to be in bad taste if they were
    (1) old and worn
    (2) too big
    (3) new and expensive

14. **What are the two standards by which Reilly measured others?**

    (1) politeness and generosity

    (2) theology and geometry

    (3) intelligence and physical strength

15. **Reilly is probably a man who**

    (1) likes to blend in with others

    (2) lives by his own standards, however unusual they may be

    (3) accepts the varieties of human behavior easily

Check your answers on page 185.

Check your answers on page 185.

Lesson 17

Setting (Fiction)

There is a difference if a story takes place in a castle two hundred years ago or on a bus today. We expect different things from people in two such different locations.

Setting is the time and the place of the action in a story. The setting of a story—or the reaction of the characters to the setting—offers clues about the characters.

As you read a passage, watch for descriptions of and clues about the setting—the room, the building, the town, the place, the time of year, the time in history. Think about what the setting means to the characters or shows about the characters. Think about the way the characters react to the setting.

TRY THIS

The following passage comes from a short story. Think about the way the boy reacts to the things he sees on the shelves. Then answer the questions that come after the passage.

     The store in which the Justice of the Peace's court was sitting smelled of cheese. The boy, crouched on his nail keg at the back of the crowded room, knew he smelled cheese, and more: from where he sat he could see the ranked shelves close-packed with the solid, squat,

(5) dynamic shapes of tin cans whose labels his stomach read, not from the lettering which meant nothing to his mind but from the scarlet devils and the silver curve of fish—this, the cheese which he knew he smelled coming in **intermittent** gusts momentary and brief between the other constant one, the smell and sense just a little of fear because mostly of

(10) despair and grief, the old fierce pull of blood. He could not see the table where the Justice sat and before which his father and his father's

The store in which the Justice of the Peace's court was sitting may have looked something like this store.

enemy (*our enemy* he thought in that despair; *ourn! mine and hisn both! He's my father!*) stood, but he could hear them, the two of them that is, because his father had said no word yet:

(15)   "But what proof have you, Mr. Harris?"

From "Barn Burning" by William Faulkner.

---

intermittent: stopping and starting

Where does the action take place?
(1) **in a store**
(2) **in a court house**
(3) **in a barn**

What is the boy sitting on? _____

What is about to begin?
(1) **a shopping expedition**
(2) **a fight**
(3) **a trial**

When does the action in the passage take place?
(1) in the past
(2) in the present
(3) in the future

How does the boy know what is in the cans on the shelves?
(1) He reads the labels on the cans.
(2) He looks at the pictures on the labels.
(3) He smells the contents of the cans.

From the way the boy knows what's in the cans, you can infer that
(1) he's never been to school
(2) he's a top student
(3) he hasn't been taught to read

The action takes place in a store—Choice (1).

As Line 2 says, the boy is sitting on a keg of nails.

A trial is about to begin—Choice (3)—which you learn in the first sentence because *the Justice of the Peace's court was sitting* in the store.

You can infer that the action takes place in the past—Choice (1)—because of two practices that are no longer common today: the Justice is holding court in a store, and nails are kept in a keg.

As Lines 5–7 say, the boy knows what's in the cans by looking at the pictures—Choice (2).

You can infer that the boy hasn't been taught to read—Choice (3)—because he identifies the contents of the can through pictures, not by reading the labels. The author uses the setting in the store to let you know that the boy can't read. You cannot make any inferences about the boy's schooling or standing in school.

EXERCISE 17

Read the next three passages and answer the questions about their settings and the effect those settings have on the characters.

Questions 1 to 5 refer to the following paragraph from a novel. Watch for clues early in the paragraph that help identify the setting.

When the two boys entered this humble but impressive building, they entered an area of **profound** and almost frightening silence. It seemed as if even the walls had become speechless, and the floor and the tables, as if silence had **engulfed** everything in the building. There
(5) were old men reading newspapers. There were town philosophers.

There were high school boys and girls doing research, but everyone was hushed, because they were seeking wisdom. They were near books. They were trying to find out. Lionel not only whispered, he moved on tiptoe. Lionel whispered because he was under the impression that it (10) was out of respect for books, not consideration for readers. Ulysses followed him, also on tiptoe, and they explored the library, each finding many treasures, Lionel—books, and Ulysses—people. Lionel didn't read books and he hadn't come to the public library to get any for himself. He just liked to see them—the thousands of them. He pointed out a (15) whole row of shelved books to his friend and then he whispered, "All of these—and these. And these. Here's a red one. All these. There's a green one. All these."

From *The Human Comedy* by William Saroyan.

profound: very deep
engulfed: swallowed up

1. What kind of building do Lionel and Ulysses explore? _____

2. Lines 1–4 emphasize what about that building?

    (1) its size
    (2) its silence
    (3) the number of people in it

3. What is it in the setting that makes Lionel whisper?

    (1) the hush
    (2) the people
    (3) the books

4. The treasure Ullysses finds as he and Lionel explore the building shows that he is interested in

    (1) people
    (2) books
    (3) wisdom

5. Which of the following best describes Lionel's feeling about the setting?

    (1) indifference
    (2) great respect
    (3) fear

Questions 6 to 10 refer to the following paragraph from a novel about a man who takes his family away from the United States to make a new, uncorrupted home for themselves.

Seven pelicans with dark freckled feathers flew low over the green sea in formation like a squadron of hedge clippers. Father said, "I hate those birds." There were gulls and vultures, too. "There's something about a coast that attracts scavengers," he said. There was a cow on (5) the beach, and railway boxcars on the pier, and the low town of La Ceiba looked yellow and jammed. Hundreds of men met our ship, not to welcome us but to quarrel with each other. Everything was backwards here. Father said, "You kids can go on ahead—you've got your knapsacks," but we were so alarmed by the heat and noise we waited (10) for him to finish with the passport official and load his tools and seed-bags into a black man's cart. Then we followed with Mother, who seemed to be holding her breath.

From *The Mosquito Coast* by Paul Theroux.

6. Which of the following is the setting for the paragraph?

    (1) a ship at sea
    (2) a quiet beach
    (3) a bustling seaport

7. The hundreds of men mentioned in the paragraph were

    (1) welcoming
    (2) tall
    (3) quarrelsome

8. What two things about the setting bothered the children?

    _____ and _____

9. The writer says that the mother *seemed to be holding her breath.* This suggests that something in the setting

    (1) made her nervous
    (2) smelled bad
    (3) made it hard for her to breathe

10. How did the setting make the children and the mother feel toward their future in that place?

    (1) enthusiastic
    (2) anxious
    (3) indifferent

Questions 11 to 15 refer to the following paragraph from a short story. You already read an earlier passage from the story on pages 120–121. Red Sam is the owner of a business called The Tower. Bailey is the grandmother's son, and June Star is Bailey's daughter.

Inside, The Tower was a long dark room with a counter at one end and tables at the other and dancing space in the middle. They all sat down at a board table next to the nickelodeon and Red Sam's wife, a tall burnt-brown woman with hair and eyes lighter than her skin, came and

(5) took their order. The children's mother put a dime in the machine and played "The Tennessee Waltz," and the grandmother said that tune always made her want to dance. She asked Bailey if he would like to dance but he only glared at her. He didn't have a naturally sunny disposition like she did and trips made him nervous. The

(10) grandmother's brown eyes were very bright. She swayed her head from side to side and pretended she was dancing in her chair. June Star said play something she could tap to so the children's mother put in another dime and played a fast number and June Star stepped out onto the dance floor and did her tap routine.

(15)   "Ain't she cute?" Red Sam's wife said, leaning over the counter. "Would you like to come be my little girl?"

    "No I certainly wouldn't," June Star said. "I wouldn't live in a broken-down place like this for a million bucks!" and she ran back to the table.

(20)   "Ain't she cute?" the woman repeated, stretching her mouth politely.

    "Arn't you ashamed?" hissed the grandmother.

From "A Good Man Is Hard to Find" by Flannery O'Connor.

11. The word *nickelodeon* in Line 3 refers to

(1) a computer game
(2) a television
(3) a coin-operated record player

12. How much did the children's mother pay each time she used the nickelodeon?

(1) 5 cents
(2) 10 cents
(3) 25 cents

13. The time in which the passage is set is most likely the

(1) past
(2) present
(3) future

14. The Tower—the place in which the action is set—is most likely a

(1) restaurant
(2) dance hall
(3) bar

15. What June Star said to Red Sam's wife gives the impression that The Tower was

    (1) very classy
    (2) rather run down
    (3) quite expensive

Check your answers on page 186.

Mood and Tone (Fiction)

Mood, in writing, is an expression of a state of mind or an emotion. The mood in a passage says something about the characters and something about the author's attitude toward his subject. Mood can range from the happiest of emotions to terror. Part of the enjoyment of literature is being caught up in the mood a writer creates.

Tone is the way an author expresses a mood. Tone is the style a writer chooses. These two statements mean about the same thing: "No way, you fool!" and "I'm sorry, but I really can't." The tones of the statements are very different, however. The first implies impatience and irritability. The second implies politeness.

As you read a passage, pay attention to the mood. Ask yourself what the writer is trying to do by choosing to express his or her story with a certain tone.

TRY THIS

The following paragraph is the beginning of a short story. In this paragraph you do not learn the characters' names, but you do learn something about one of the characters from the mood. Read the paragraph carefully. Watch for words that reveal something of the character of the person referred to as "he." Then answer the questions that follow.

> All the optimism that had colored his flight from the city was gone now, had vanished the evening of the first day, as they drove north through the dark stands of redwood. Now, the rolling pasture land, the cows, the isolated farmhouses of western Washington
> (5) seemed to hold out nothing for him, nothing he really wanted. He had expected something different.

From "How About This?" by Raymond Carver.

What feeling did the character have as he left the city? _____

What happened to that feeling? _____

What does the landscape and the scenery of western Washington

offer the character? _____

Which of the following best describes the feeling or mood of the
passage?

(1) enthusiasm

(2) disappointment

(3) hope

When the character left the city, he had a feeling of optimism.
That feeling vanished.

The landscape and scenery seemed to offer nothing for him.

Disappointment—Choice (2)—is closest to the mood of the
passage. The character seems to have lost all hope. When the author
says that the character *had expected something different*, the
author reveals the character's disappointment.

Notice the effect of the words *dark* (Line 3) and *isolated* (Line 4)
and the repetition of the word *nothing* in Line 5. These words add to
the atmosphere of disappointment.

Read the next three passages and answer the questions. Some of the questions are about things in a passage that help to create its mood or tone. Others are about the mood or tone, itself.

Questions 1 to 5 refer to the following passage, which has quite a different feeling from disappointment. The author has written the passage with Adam, the husband of Eve, as the narrator. Adam, according to the book of Genesis in the Old Testament, was the first man. He and Eve once lived in the Garden of Eden. Think about the ways the author creates the tone of the passage.

A large number of people have expressed curiosity as to how Eve and I like residing out of Eden. The answer is very simple. We like it fine.

(5) I began as a farm boy, so the thorns and thistles of the "outer world" are not news to me. We thoroughly enjoyed our years in Eden, but now that they are over we find many things to enjoy elsewhere. Pleasant as it was, Eden always had the disadvantage for me personally of being a little too lush and orderly. As the saying goes, I like some grit to my mash.

(10) So many contradictory accounts of what happened have been published that I think the time has come to set the record straight. Now that my grandson Enoch has builded a city of the same name, I know there is a firm watertight place where the records can be kept. I think it is very important, whether or not it causes embarrassment in Heaven,

(15) for the First Man to set down in his own words his side of the story so that the generations succeeding him in this world can understand their present condition and why things are the way they are.

When the matter first came up of eating of the tree of knowledge of good and evil, I consulted with Eve and with the serpent and their

(20) **consensus** seemed to be that it could do no harm and might do a lot of good. It is easy to identify mistakes in hindsight, but at the time this was the best available information I could get, and it was my responsibility to act upon it. And I did.

The following day, God came to me and asked, "Hast thou eaten of

(25) the tree, whereof I commanded thee that thou shouldest not eat?"

I thought this was a curious question, since if He were **omniscient** as supposed He must have already known that I certainly had. But I have never had any trouble keeping the reins on my temper. With the utmost patience and courtesy I explained the situation.

(30)   When I was done, He simply told me, "In the sweat of thy face shalt thou eat bread, till thou return unto the ground." I felt lucky at that, since what He said to Eve and the serpent was far worse.

We wasted no time getting out, once the circumstances had become definite. I expected no fanfare, so it was one of the deeply moving

(35) experiences of my life to see all the **cherubim** waving goodbye with their flaming swords. I had not in any way asked them to do this. It was a truly spontaneous demonstration.

From "Mr. Ex-Resident" by John Updike.

> *consensus:* general agreement
> *omniscient:* all knowing
> *cherubim:* a type of angel

1. What is Adam's criticism of Eden?

   (1) He didn't like the thorns.
   (2) The food was gritty.
   (3) It was too lush and orderly.

2. Adam refers to himself both as a farm boy and as

   (1) First Man
   (2) God
   (3) Enoch

3. When Adam says he wants to tell *his side of the story* (Line 15) even if *it causes embarrassment in Heaven* (Line 14), his attitude seems a bit

   (1) sad
   (2) irreverent
   (3) fearful

4. Compared to the way God speaks in Lines 24–25 and 30–31, Adam's tone throughout the passage is more

   (1) formal
   (2) biblical
   (3) informal

5. The tone of the passage is

   (1) serious
   (2) angry
   (3) humorous

Questions 6 to 10 refer to the following passage from a short story. Think about the relationship between the two main characters.

"That jerk," Wayne said.

"Who?" she said. "Who are you talking about?" she said, laying down her spoon.

"The waiter," Wayne said. "The waiter. The newest and the

(5) dumbest waiter in the house, and we got him."

"Eat your soup," she said. "Don't blow a gasket."

Wayne lighted a cigaret. The waiter arrived with salads and took away the soup bowls.

When they had started on the main course, Wayne said, "Well,

(10) what do you think? Is there a chance for us or not?" He looked down and arranged the napkin on his lap.

"Maybe so," she said. "There's always a chance."

"Don't give me that kind of crap," he said. "Answer me straight for a change."

(15) "Don't snap at me," she said.

"I'm asking you," he said. "Give me a straight answer," he said.

She said, "You want something signed in blood?"

He said, "That wouldn't be such a bad idea."

She said, "You listen to me! I've given you the best years of my life.

(20) The best years of my life!"

"The best years of *your* life?" he said.

"I'm thirty-six years old," she said. "Thirty-seven tonight. Tonight, right now, at this minute, I just can't say what I'm going to do. I'll just have to see," she said.

(25) "I don't care what you do," he said.

"Is that true?" she said.

He threw down his fork and tossed his napkin on the table.

"Are you finished?" she asked pleasantly. "Let's have coffee and dessert. We'll have a nice dessert. Something good."

(30) She finished everything on her plate.

From "Signals" by Raymond Carver.

6. What is the setting of this passage?

    (1) a car

    (2) a restaurant

    (3) Wayne's house

7. Why does Wayne say *Don't give me that kind of crap* in Line 13?

    (1) He is upset about the bad service.

    (2) He doesn't like the main course.

    (3) He is angry because the woman didn't answer his question directly.

8. When the woman says, *Don't snap at me* (Line 15), she is responding to Wayne's

   (1) impatience with her
   (2) complaints about the food
   (3) rudeness to the waiter

9. What is special about the day on which the passage is set?

   (1) It is the woman's birthday.
   (2) It is Wayne and the woman's wedding anniversary.
   (3) Wayne has chosen this day to propose to the woman.

10. Which of the following best describes the mood in most of this passage?

    (1) sadness
    (2) celebration
    (3) irritation

Questions 11 to 15 refer to the following passage from a novel. Think about the way the writer creates the tone in this passage.

The sounds of the rodeo around me fade in my concentration. There's a drone in my ears that blocks out everything else, pasts and futures and long-range worries. The horse and I are held in a vise, a wind-up toy that has been turned one twist too many, a spring coiled
(5) beyond its limit.

"Now!" I cry, aloud or to myself I don't know. Everything has boiled down to this instant. There's nothing in the world except the hand of the gate judge, lowering in slow motion to the catch that contains us. I see each of his fingers clearly, separately, as they fold
(10) around the lever, I see the muscles in his forearm harden as he begins to push down.

I never expected the music.

Wheeling and spinning, tilting and beating, my breath the song, the horse the dance. Time is gone. All the ordinary ways of things, the
(15) gettings from here to there, the one and twos, forgot. The crowd is color, the whirl of a spun top. The noises blend into a waving band that flies around us like a ribbon on a string. Beneath me four feet dance, pounding and leaping and turning and stomping. My legs flap like wings. I sail above, first to one side, then the other, remembering more
(20) than feeling the slaps of our bodies together. Things happen faster than understanding, faster than ideas. I'm a bird coasting, shot free into the music, spiraling into a place without bones or weight.

I'm on the ground. Unmoving. The heels of my hands sunk in the dust of the arena. My knees sore. Dizzy. Back in time. I shake sense into
(25) my head, listen as the loudspeaker brays.

"Twenty-four seconds for the young cowboy from eastern Montana. Nice try, son. Hoka-hay."

From *A Yellow Raft in Blue Water* by Michael Dorris.

11. The passage describes

    (1) cowboys at work
    (2) riding a horse in a rodeo
    (3) how to train horses

12. The words *concentration, vise, wind-up toy,* and *a spring coiled* in the first paragraph help to create a mood of

    (1) playfulness
    (2) tension
    (3) humor

13. In the fourth paragraph (Lines 13–22), the author describes a variety of

    (1) movements
    (2) sounds
    (3) sights

14. The mood created by the fourth paragraph is one of

    (1) excitement
    (2) defeat
    (3) sorrow

15. What has happened just before the paragraph that starts on Line 23?

    (1) The judge has thrown the rider out of the contest.
    (2) The rider has been thrown from the horse.
    (3) The rider has wakened from a dream.

Check your answers on page 187.

Lesson 19

Analyzing Drama

You have already read passages from several plays in this book. In this chapter you will learn some of the special vocabulary that goes with drama.

A piece of drama or a play is similar to a story or novel. There is a **setting**—the time and location where the action takes place. There is a **plot**—the series of events that make up the main story. There is usually a **theme**—a main point. And there is **characterization**—the representation of human character.

Sometimes there is even a narrator—a character who fills in missing pieces in the action of a play. More often, the characters themselves supply these details. Most of what goes on in a play occurs in the dialogue between the characters.

The author of a play is called the **playwright,** and the characters make up the **cast.**

The written version of a play is called a **script.** If a play is written for the movies, it is usually called a **screenplay.** If it is for television, it is called a **teleplay.**

The instructions a playwright gives to the actors are called the **stage directions**—since most plays are meant to be performed on a stage.

Plays, like short stories and novels, vary in length. A play can be written as one continuous piece or one **act.** Plays can also be written in several acts, each of which may be divided into **scenes.**

TRY THIS

Below is an outline of the play *Come Back, Little Sheba* by William Inge. Read the outline and answer the questions that follow.

SCENE
  An old house in a run-down neighborhood of a Midwestern city.
Act One
  Scene I   Morning in late spring.
  Scene II   The same evening, after supper.
Act Two
  Scene I   The following morning.
  Scene II   Late afternoon the same day.
  Scene III 5:30 the next morning.
  Scene IV   Morning, a week later.

What is the setting of the play? _____

The play is divided into how many acts? _____

Act One is divided into how many scenes? _____

Act Two is divided into how many scenes? _____

About how much time is covered by the action of the entire play?
  (1) one day
  (2) a couple of days
  (3) a little more than a week
  (4) a couple of months

The setting of the play is an old house in a run-down neighborhood of a Midwestern city.

The play is divided into two acts.

Act One has two scenes, and Act Two has four scenes.

The action in the play takes place in a little more than a week—Choice (3). From Scene I of the first act to Scene III of the second act, two days and one morning pass. The last scene takes place a week later. So approximately nine days pass in the course of the play.

As you read a play, try to imagine hearing actors say the dialogue out loud. Pay close attention to the stage directions, which are usually written in parentheses ( ) or brackets [ ]. These offer important clues to the feelings expressed in the play and the action that may appear on the stage.

EXERCISE 19

Read the next three passages from plays and answer the questions about them. The questions will help you to analyze the passages.

Questions 1 to 5 refer to the following passage from a teleplay. It was adapted from a famous novel, *The Old Man and the Sea* by Ernest Hemingway. The action takes place on a beach in Cuba. Santiago is an old fisherman, and Angela is his daughter. The character Lopez, who is referred to, runs the local cafe.

SANTIAGO'S SHACK, *night. Santiago is asleep in the chair outside. Angela, his daughter, arrives and takes some food inside. She comes back outside and puts a blanket around his shoulders. He opens his eyes.*

(5) ANGELA: The sun's gone down.

SANTIAGO: You were very quiet.

ANGELA: I brought you some fruit.

SANTIAGO: Thank you.

ANGELA: Momma's picture is not on the wall.

(10) SANTIAGO: I put it on the shelf where I see it less. It makes me too lonely.

ANGELA: Come inside.

SANTIAGO: I'm very comfortable out here.

ANGELA: Papa, come inside.

(15) SANTIAGO (*resigned*): You won't stay long?

ANGELA: No.

SANTIAGO: Good. (*He takes his chair inside the shack.*)

ANGELA (*follows him*): You can't live like this. Eighty-four days without a fish. Lopez's brother works in a bodega on the same street

(20) where we live. So even in Havana we know about Santiago's bad luck. Papa, we have an extra room. Things are going well. I talked it over with Tomas. You'll come to us. You'll have your own room. You can read your paper. You can listen to the radio. It's time now. People will say I'm a bad daughter, leaving you like this, living like a hermit with

(25) a dirt floor.

SANTIAGO: It's enough for me.

ANGELA: Ay, you're like a bad child, stubborn. For years now, I've said, please, Papa, leave here, come to Havana. And you always say, no, I go out every day. I'm a fisherman. But God is saying it's time. He doesn't

(30) give you any more fish. He wants you to come to me in Havana.

SANTIAGO: You know what God is thinking?

ANGELA: He doesn't give you any more fish. He thinks you are too old.

SANTIAGO: He will give me a fish, a great fish.

ANGELA: When?

(35) SANTIAGO: Tomorrow.

ANGELA: And if not?

SANTIAGO: The next day.

ANGELA: And if you die, the shame will be on me.

SANTIAGO: There is no shame for a man to die the way he lived.

(40) ANGELA: Papa, please. I love you.

SANTIAGO: Then let me be. A room in the city with a radio? A seat in the park in the sun? Nothing to do with these hands, with these arms, with these eyes. You have a good husband. Thank Tomas for his good thoughts. But I will stay here and look for fish.

(45) ANGELA: I'm sorry to say this, but you are too old.

SANTIAGO (*angry*): No.

From *The Old Man and the Sea*, a teleplay by Roger O. Hirson
based on the novel by Ernest Hemingway.

1. The setting of this scene suggests that Santiago is

   (1) very rich

   (2) financially comfortable

   (3) rather poor

2. Apparently Santiago is

    (1) married

    (2) single

    (3) widowed

3. Why has Angela come to visit her father?

    (1) just to say hello

    (2) to complain about her husband

    (3) to convince her father to move in with her in Havana

4. In Line 39 Santiago says, *There is no shame for a man to die the way he lived.* He probably means that he

    (1) is too old to learn new tricks

    (2) would rather die working as a fisherman than move to the city

    (3) would like to die in peace and his daughter should leave him alone

5. At the end of the passage, Santiago feels

    (1) lonely

    (2) angry

    (3) old

Questions 6 to 10 refer to the following passage from a play called *The Subject Was Roses.* The scene takes place in an apartment in the Bronx in May 1946. Timmy has just returned home from serving in the army. John is his father. The dialogue is the only important thing here. There are no clues to the action in stage directions.

    TIMMY: Want to hear the bravest thing I ever did?

    JOHN: Yes.

    TIMMY: The first night we were in combat I slept with my boots off.

    JOHN: Go on.

(5)   **TIMMY:** That's right.

    JOHN: You slept with your boots off?

    TIMMY: Doesn't sound like much, does it?

    JOHN: Not offhand.

    TIMMY: The fellows who eventually cracked up were all guys who

(10)   couldn't sleep. If I hadn't decided to take my boots off I'd have ended up being one of them.

    JOHN: I see.

    TIMMY: Want to know the smartest thing I did?

    JOHN: Sure.

(15)   **TIMMY:** I never volunteered. One day the lieutenant bawled me out for

it. I said, "Sir, if there's anything you want me to do, you tell me and
I'll do it. But if you wait for me to volunteer you'll wait forever."

JOHN: What did he say to that?

TIMMY: Nothing printable. The fact is I wasn't a very good soldier, Pop.

(20) JOHN: You did everything they asked you.

TIMMY: The good ones do more. You'd have been a good one.

JOHN: What makes you say that?

TIMMY: I can tell.

JOHN: Well, thanks.

(25) TIMMY: You're welcome.

JOHN: It's one of the big regrets of my life that I was never in the
service.

TIMMY: I know.

JOHN: The day World War One was declared I went to the recruiting

(30)   office. When they learned I was the sole support of the family, they
turned me down.

TIMMY: I know.

From *The Subject Was Roses* by Frank D. Gilroy.

6. What does Timmy say were the bravest and the smartest things
that he did? _____ and _____

7. Which of the following best explains the importance of Timmy's
sleeping with his boots off during combat?

   (1) He wanted the opportunity to go against authority.
   (2) He knew it was dangerous, but he had to do it to survive
       emotionally.
   (3) He wanted to make his father proud of him.

8. Which of the following best summarizes the way Timmy thinks
about himself as a soldier?

   (1) He is proud that he survived.
   (2) He thinks that he was one of the good ones.
   (3) He knows he got away with doing the least he could.

9. In the second part of Line 21, Timmy says something about his
father. Does he express a fact or an opinion? _____

10. Why was John turned down as a soldier in World War One?

   (1) He failed the physical examination.
   (2) He was too young.
   (3) He was the only support for his family.

Questions 11 to 15 refer to the following passage from a play called *Fences*. The characters are Troy Maxon, a garbage man, and his wife, Rose. The time is the fifties.

Troy is a bitter man. Although he was talented, he could not play baseball in the major leagues because of his color. He has been seeing a woman named Alberta.

TROY: What you want from me, Rose?

ROSE: I want you to act like my husband.

TROY: You ain't wanted me to act like your husband last night. You ain't wanted no part of me.

(5) ROSE: You going down there to see her ain't you. You going down there to be with her and then wanna come crawl in my bed.

TROY: I ain't gonna see nobody. I told you what I was gonna do.

ROSE: I ain't gonna stand for this too much longer. You living on borrowed time with me.

(10) TROY: My whole life I been living on borrowed time.

ROSE: Troy, I want you to come home tomorrow after work.

TROY: Rose . . . I don't mess up my pay. You know that now. I takes my pay and I gives it to you. I don't have no money but what you give me back. I just want to have a little time to myself . . . a little time to

(15) enjoy life.

ROSE: Troy, I am you wife! What about me? When's my time to enjoy life?

TROY: I don't know what to tell you, Rose. I just don't know what to tell you. [*The telephone is heard ringing inside the house.* ROSE *exits into*

(20) *the house.* TROY *sits down on the steps of the porch. Presently* ROSE *returns.*]

ROSE: Troy. . . . There somebody on the phone from the hospital. They want to talk to you. They say it's about Alberta. [TROY *exits into the house.* ROSE *stands apprehensive, waiting, preparing herself for any*

(25) *possible scenario.* TROY *enters, pained and downcast.*]

ROSE: Troy, what is it? What's the matter?

TROY: Alberta died having the baby.

ROSE: No! . . . She's too young to die, Troy.

TROY: Death don't know nobody's age. Sometimes I don't even think he

(30) knows their name. The Bible say he comes like a thief in the night. You don't know how many times he comes before he finds you home.

ROSE: What about the baby? Is the baby alright?

TROY: Baby's alright. It's a girl. They say it's healthy.

ROSE: I'm sorry, Troy.

(35) TROY: Yeah, so am I. Sorry ain't gonna do nothing.

From *Fences* by August Wilson.

11. The setting for this scene seems to be

    (1) outside Troy and Rose's house
    (2) in a hospital
    (3) at Alberta's house

12. What does Rose want at the beginning of the scene?

    (1) for Troy to give her more money
    (2) a divorce
    (3) for her and Troy to patch up their marriage

13. When Rose says *I ain't gonna stand for this too much longer* (Line 8), she is referring to Troy's

    (1) constant complaining
    (2) affair with another woman
    (3) unwillingness to let her have a good time

14. When Rose insists that Troy come home the next day after work, Troy

    (1) promises to come home
    (2) ignores Rose
    (3) says he needs time to himself

15. At the beginning of the passage, the mood is angry. At the end it is

    (1) still angry
    (2) calm
    (3) sad

Check your answers on page 187.

Lesson 20

Analyzing Poetry

On a page, poetry doesn't *look* like prose (fiction and nonfiction). Poetry is written in individual lines that are usually not as wide as a page. Sometimes the lines are divided into groups called **stanzas.** For an example, look ahead to the poem "South End" on pages 145–146. It is divided into five stanzas.

Poetry also doesn't *sound* like prose. Sometimes poetry **rhymes**—that is, the final words of some lines sound similar to the final words of other lines. Poetry usually sounds more musical than prose, too. Poets choose words not just for their meanings but also for their sounds.

Figurative Language

Poetry is different from prose in another way. Poetry is written with more **figurative language.** Figurative language does not mean literally what it says. It means more than what appears on the surface. Following are some examples of figurative language often used in poetry.

A **simile** is a comparison between two things using the words *like* or *as.* "Her eyes are like stars" is a simile.

A **metaphor** is used to say that one thing *is* something else. "Life is a dream" is a metaphor.

Personification means giving human or animal qualities to things. "The moon guided us through the night" is an example of personification. The moon cannot, of course, act as a guide in a literal sense. But the moon's light, position, or movement can serve as a guide.

Reading a Poem

Poetry requires careful reading. It's a good idea to read poems more than once. If you can, read poems out loud. Reading a poem out loud gives you a chance to appreciate the sounds of the words the poet uses. It also gives you a chance to think about the meaning of the words and about the images the poet creates.

Remember to pay close attention to the title. The title is often a key to the meaning of the figurative language in the poem.

TRY THIS

Read the following, which is the first stanza of a poem. Then answer the questions.

SLIPPING

Age comes to my father as a slow
slipping: the leg that weakens, will
barely support him, the curtain of mist
that falls over one eye. Years, like
(5) pickpockets, lift his concentration,
memory, fine sense of direction. The car,
as he drives, drifts from lane to lane
like a raft on a river, speeds and slows
for no reason, keeps missing turns.

By Joan Aleshire.

Which of the following best tells the topic of this stanza?
(1) fathers
(2) aging
(3) driving

How does the poet say age comes to her father? _____

The poet says that years are like _____

The word *lift* in Line 5 probably means
(1) improve
(2) steal
(3) raise

The poet compares the car driven by her father to a _____

The topic of this stanza is aging, Choice (2).

The poet uses a simile to say that age comes *as a slow slipping*. Notice that *Slipping* is the title of the poem.

The poet uses another simile and says that years are like *pickpockets.*

The word *lift* probably means steal, Choice (2). The poet has just mentioned pickpockets, who "lift" wallets.

The poet uses yet another simile when she compares the car driven by her father to *a raft on a river.*

NOW TRY THIS

Read the next poem and answer the questions that follow it. Pay attention to the rhyme in the poem and watch for examples of personification.

SOUTH END
The benches are broken, the grassplots brown and bare,
the laurels dejected, in this neglected square.
Dogs couple undisturbed. The roots of trees
heave up the bricks in the sidewalk as they please.

(5) Nobody collects the papers from the grass,
nor the dead matches, nor the broken glass.
The elms are old and shabby; the houses, around,
stare lazily through paintless shutters at forgotten ground.

Out of the dusty fountain, with the dust,
(10) the leaves fly up like birds on a sudden gust.
The leaves fly up like birds, and the papers flap,
or round the legs of benches wrap and unwrap.

Here, for the benefit of some secret sense,
warm-autumn-afternoon finds permanence.
(15) No one will hurry, or wait too long, or die:
All is serenity, under a serene sky.

Dignity shines in old brick and old dirt,
in elms and houses now hurt beyond all hurt.
A broken square where little lives or moves;
these are the city's earliest and tenderest loves.

By Conrad Aiken.

What is the topic of the poem?
(1) nature
(2) a city neighborhood
(3) a farm

In each stanza, the last word of the first line rhymes with the last word of
(1) the second line
(2) the third line
(3) the fourth line

In each stanza, the last word of the third line rhymes with the last word of
(1) the first line
(2) the second line
(3) the fourth line

A laurel (Line 2) is a kind of tree. The poet personifies laurels when he describes them with what word? _____
The poet personifies the *roots of trees* (Line 3). **What does he say they do?** _____

The topic of the poem is a city neighborhood. **The title is a clue.** The words *neglected square* (Line 2), *fountain* (Line 9), and *benches* (Line 12) also suggest things in a city.

In each stanza, the last word of the first line rhymes with the last word of the second line. For example, in the first stanza, *bare* rhymes with *square*.

The last word of the third line in each stanza rhymes with the last word of the fourth line. For example, also in the first stanza, *trees* rhymes with *please*.

The poet personifies laurels when he says they are *dejected*. To be dejected is a human quality, not a quality of trees.

The poet says that the roots of trees *heave up the bricks in the sidewalk as they please.*

Before you go on, read the last poem again. Look for similes, metaphors, and examples of personification. Poets use these types of figurative language to make us look at the world differently, to make us look more carefully.

Read the next three poems and answer the questions about them. The questions will help you to analyze the poems.

Questions 1 to 5 refer to the following poem, which mentions stars in each stanza. As you read, think about what other subject, besides stars, the poet is describing.

THE MORE LOVING ONE

Looking up at the stars, I know quite well
That, for all they care, I can go to hell,
But on earth indifference is the least
We have to dread from man or beast.

(5) How should we like it were stars to burn
With a passion for us we could not return?
If equal affection cannot be,
Let the more loving one be me.

Admirer as I think I am
(10) Of stars that do not give a damn,
I cannot, now I see them, say
I missed one terribly all day.

Were all stars to disappear or die,
I should learn to look at an empty sky
(15) And feel its total dark sublime,
Though this might take me a little time.

By W. H. Auden.

1. The poem is divided into how many stanzas? _____

2. The last word of the first line in each stanza rhymes with the last word in what other line? _____

3. What has the poet personified in the first stanza?

    (1) stars

    (2) earth

    (3) beasts

4. The poet writes about stars in order to say something about

    (1) astronomy

    (2) nature

    (3) love

5. Which of the following best summarizes the meaning of the last stanza of the poem?

    (1) Some things are simply too hard to adjust to.

    (2) Although it would be hard, the poet could get used to starless nights and a life without loving relationships.

    (3) We cannot live without stars any more than we can live without others.

Questions 6 to 11 refer to the following poem. Think about the narrator, the person who is telling the story of the poem.

MY PAPA'S WALTZ

The whiskey on your breath
Could make a small boy dizzy;
But I held on like death:
Such waltzing was not easy.

(5) We romped until the pans
Slid from the kitchen shelf;
My mother's **countenance**
Could not unfrown itself.

The hand that held my wrist
(10) Was battered on one knuckle;
At every step you missed
My right ear scraped a buckle.

You beat time on my head
With a palm caked hard by dirt,
Then waltzed me off to bed
(15) Still clinging to your shirt.

By Theodore Roethke.

countenance: the look on a face

6. The last word in the first line of each stanza rhymes with the last word of which other line in the stanza? _____

7. The poem describes

    (1) a child's dream
    (2) a mother's appearance
    (3) a child dancing with his father

8. Who is the narrator of the poem?

    (1) the child
    (2) the father
    (3) the mother

9. Lines 7 and 8 probably mean that the mother

    (1) didn't approve of dancing
    (2) was worried for her child's safety
    (3) was not the friendly type

10. The buckle mentioned in Line 12 was probably

    (1) on the father's belt
    (2) hanging from a wall
    (3) attached to the child's clothes

11. The narrator's feeling is best described as

    (1) complete joy
    (2) happiness mixed with sadness
    (3) fondness together with some fear

Questions 12 to 15 refer to the following sonnet (a poem in 14 lines) by perhaps the greatest writer of English, William Shakespeare, who lived from 1564 to 1616. The language is not modern, but it is not too difficult.

MY MISTRESS' EYES

My mistress' eyes are nothing like the sun;
Coral is far more red than her lips' red:
If snow be white, why then her breasts are **dun**;
If hairs be wires, black wires grow on her head.
(5) I have seen **roses damasked**, red and white,
But no such roses see I in her cheeks;
And in some perfumes is there more delight
Than in the breath that from my mistress **reeks**.
I love to hear her speak—yet well I know

(10) That music hath a far more pleasing sound;
      I grant I never saw a goddess go—
      My mistress, when she walks, treads on the ground.
            And yet, by heaven, I think my love as rare
            As any she belied with false compare.

By William Shakespeare.

> *dun:* a dull, grayish brown
> *roses damasked:* fragrant cultivated roses
> *reeks:* escapes; the word also suggests an offensive smell
> *belied:* misrepresented, gave a false idea of

12. In this poem there are several "negative comparisons." What does the poet say each of the following things about his mistress is NOT like?

   (a) her eyes _____

   (b) her lips _____

   (c) her breasts _____

   (d) her cheeks _____

   (e) her breath _____

   (f) her voice _____

13. The first twelve lines give the impression that the poet's mistress is

   (1) unusually beautiful
   (2) not so special
   (3) unkind to him

14. At the end you can conclude that the poet

   (1) hopes to find a more pleasing mistress
   (2) is very much in love with his mistress
   (3) plans to leave his mistress

15. The poet's tone through most of the poem is full of
   (1) sadness
   (2) regret
   (3) humor

Check your answers on page 188.

This section of the unit contains readings from literature and commentary on the arts. These readings can help you prepare for the GED in at least two ways. You can use them to
- expand your general knowledge of literature and the arts
- practice the reading skills covered in Units 1, 2, and 3

Directions: Read the next passages and answer the questions that follow each.

Questions 1 to 5 refer to the following passage from a reflection about the 1930s childhood of the writer Kurt Vonnegut. In this passage he describes a woman who was an important influence on him.

Phoebe Hurty hired me to write copy for ads about teenage clothes. I had to wear the clothes I praised. That was part of the job. And I became friends
(5) with her two sons, who were my age. I was over at their house all the time.
She would talk **bawdily** to me and her sons, and to our girlfriends when we brought them around. She was
(10) funny. She was liberating. She taught us to be impolite in conversation not only about sexual matters, but about American history and famous heroes, about the distribution of wealth,
(15) about school, about everything.
I now make my living by being impolite. I am clumsy at it. I keep trying to imitate the impoliteness which was so graceful in Phoebe
(20) Hurty. I think now that grace was easier for her than it is for me because of the mood of the Great Depression. She believed what so many Americans believed then: that the nation would
(25) be happy and just and rational when prosperity came.
I never hear that word anymore: *Prosperity.* It used to be a synonym for *Paradise.* And Phoebe Hurty was
(30) able to give shape to an American paradise.

Now her sort of impoliteness is fashionable. But nobody believes anymore in a new American paradise.
(35) I sure miss Phoebe Hurty.

From *Wampeters, Foma & Granfalloons* by Kurt Vonnegut.

bawdily: using coarse language

1. How did the author come to know to Phoebe Hurty?
   (1) He lived in her house.
   (2) He worked for her.
   (3) She was his friends' mother.

2. What did the author admire about Phoebe Hurty?
   (1) her gracefulness
   (2) her hopes for the United States after the Depression
   (3) her ideas and the way she presented them

3. Which of these statements from the passage is NOT an opinion of the author's?
   (1) I had to wear the clothes I praised.
   (2) She was funny.
   (3) Now her sort of impoliteness is fashionable.

4. One of the author's main points is that from Phoebe Hurty he learned to
   (1) question ideas and beliefs
   (2) believe in prosperity
   (3) be rude to people

151

5. The author probably thinks that children should

   (1) obey their parents in all things
   (2) learn to think for themselves
   (3) treat their elders rudely

Questions 6 to 10 refer to the following passage from a short story about someone named Anna, who is called *she* in the passage. Pay close attention to the mood and to the clues about what is happening with the characters.

She looked in the rearview mirror, but snow had covered the window; she looked to both sides. To her right, at the far end of the shopping center, the
(5) doughnut shop was open, and in front of it three cars were topped with snow. All the other stores were closed. She would be able to see headlights through the snow on the rear window,
(10) and if a cruiser came she was to go into the store, and if Wayne had not already started, she would buy cigarettes, then go out again, and if the cruiser was gone she would wait in
(15) the car; if the cruiser had stopped, she would go back into the store for matches and they would both leave. Now in the dark and heater warmth she believed all of their plan was no
(20) longer risky, but doomed, as if by leaving the car and walking across the short space through soft angling snow, Wayne had become puny, his knife a toy. So it was the wrong girl
(25) too, and the wrong man. She could not imagine him coming out with money, and she could not imagine tomorrow or later tonight or even the next minute. Stripped of history and
(30) dreams, she knew only her breathing and smoking and heartbeat and the falling snow. She stared at the long window of the drugstore, and she was startled when he came out: he was
(35) running, he was alone, he was inside, closing the door. He said *Jesus Christ* three times as she crossed the parking lot. She turned on the headlights and

slowed as she neared the highway. She
(40) did not have to stop. She moved into the right lane, and cars in the middle and left passed her.
   'A *lot*.' he said.

From "Anna" by Andre Dubus.

6. Answer the following questions about the setting in this passage.

   (a) What is the season of the year?

   _____

   (b) What is the time of day?

   _____

   (c) Where is Anna throughout most of the passage? (Give as many details as possible.) _____

7. In Lines 18–32 the author's main purpose is to show that Anna

   (1) is scared because she has lost faith in the plan she and Wayne made
   (2) thinks the plan she and Wayne made won't work because of the toy knife
   (3) now thinks that she and Wayne are not the right people for what they are doing

8. By the end of the passage, Wayne has

   (1) had a religious experience
   (2) stolen money from a store
   (3) killed someone in a store

9. The mood of the passage is one of

   (1) secrecy and betrayal
   (2) tension and fear
   (3) calm and relaxation

10. If Anna got a new job with more responsibility than she had ever had, she would probably approach the job with

   (1) a feeling of confidence
   (2) a lack of concern
   (3) worry about whether she could succeed

Questions 11 to 15 refer to the following paragraph, which comes from the book review that you read part of on page 117.

"The 1990 Buick LeSabre Owner's Manual" is strikingly different. None of it applies only to light trucks or only to some other kind of Buick. All

(5) of it is about the LeSabre. Better yet, virtually all of it is readable. Have to change a flat? "The equipment you'll need is in the trunk." Ah, but suppose you've never touched a jack in your

(10) life, aren't even sure what one looks like. The manual is prepared. It expected that. It contains 26 color photographs that **sequentially** picture the changing of a tire. (The

(15) first two are **cameo** shots of the jack and of the wheel wrench.) Each action shot is accompanied by simple directions. Typical direction: "Take off the nuts. Keep them near you." A

(20) visiting Martian, if taught English and given the manual, could probably change a LeSabre tire.

From "Getting to Know Your Synchronized Input Shaft" by Noel Perrin.

> **sequentially:** in order
> **cameo:** small and sharp

11. The author's main point is that "The 1990 Buick LeSabre Owner's Manual"
    (1) is about only one car
    (2) has helpful illustrations
    (3) is both useful and easy to read

12. Which of the following statements from the passage is a fact?
    (1) Better yet, virtually all of it is readable.
    (2) Each action shot is accompanied by simple directions.
    (3) A visiting Martian . . . could probably change a LeSabre tire.

13. In this passage the author tries to
    (1) illustrate the good points about the LeSabre manual
    (2) convince readers to buy LeSabres
    (3) explain what he likes about automobile manuals

14. The tone of this passage is
    (1) serious and deep
    (2) light and upbeat
    (3) heavy and technical

15. The author would probably least like to read
    (1) a cookbook with pictures of the steps for making something
    (2) the directions for filling out federal income tax forms
    (3) an illustrated First Aid booklet that explains things simply

Questions 16 to 20 refer to the following poem. You read part of this poem on page 144.

SLIPPING

Age comes to my father as a slow
slipping: the leg that weakens, will
barely support him, the curtain of mist
that falls over one eye. Years, like

(5) pickpockets, lift his concentration,
memory, fine sense of direction. The car,
as he drives, drifts from lane to lane
like a raft on a river, speeds and slows
for no reason, keeps missing turns.

(10) As my mother says, "He's never liked
to talk about feelings," but tonight
out walking, as I slow to match his pace—
his left leg trailing a little like
a child who keeps pulling on your hand—he says,
(15) "I love you so much." Darkness, and the sense
we always have that each visit may be
the last, have pushed away years of restraint.

A photograph taken of him teaching—
white coat, stethoscope like a pet snake
(20) around his neck, chair tipped back
against the lecture-room wall—shows
a man talking, love of his work lighting
his face—in a way we seldom saw at home.
I answer that I love him, too, but
(25) hardly knowing him, what I love
is the way reserve has slipped from
his feeling, like a screen suddenly
falling, exposing someone dressing or
washing: how wrinkles ring a bent neck,
(30) how soft and **mutable** is the usually hidden flesh.

By Joan Aleshire.

> **mutable:** capable of changing

16. Her father's stethoscope reminds the poet of
    (1) a photograph
    (2) a pet snake
    (3) a chair

17. You can infer that the poet's father is
    (1) a photographer
    (2) an athlete
    (3) a doctor

18. The author compares reserve slipping away to
    (1) a mirror breaking
    (2) a chair tipping over
    (3) a screen falling

19. The main idea the poet expresses is that she
    (1) loves that her father now expresses his feelings more than he used to
    (2) sees many signs that her father is aging
    (3) realizes that her father's work has been very important to him throughout his life

20. The mood of the poem is mainly one of
    (1) fondness
    (2) regret
    (3) sorrow

Questions 21 to 25 refer to the following passage from the play that you read part of on pages 138–139. Tom is a writer who has become interested in the fate of the old fisherman, Santiago. Mary is Tom's wife, and Manolo is a fifteen-year-old boy.

DUNE ROAD, night. Tom and Mary are walking along, parallel to the beach.

TOM: Are you bored here?
MARY: I feel at loose ends. I don't feel
(5) very useful to myself or anyone else.
TOM: I can't leave here right now.
Something is happening. I have to
find out what it is. If I don't, I'm lost.
MARY: Where does that leave me?
(10) TOM: I love you. You know that.

MARY: Do I? (*He stops, looks at her, then starts walking on.*) Where are you going?

TOM: I don't know.

(15) MARY: Wait for me. (*He stops. She joins him, and they walk along together. They see Manolo sitting on a dune, looking out to sea. They go over to him.*)

(20) TOM: May we sit with you? (*Manolo nods. They sit beside him.*) The old man is your friend?

MANOLO: We have been fishing together many times.

(25) MARY: How old is he?

MANOLO: I don't know. What difference does it make?

TOM: Will he be back?

MANOLO: Yes. And with a fish. He is a
(30) great fisherman . . . more than that. (*Silence.*) Once, when I first was in the boat with him, he hooked a marlin, one of a pair—the female, which always feeds before the male.
(35) The female fought against the line, and the male crossed and made circles. Santiago was afraid the male would cut the line with his tail, but soon Santiago **gaffed** the female and
(40) clubbed her. The male stayed by the side of the boat. Then, while the old man was clearing the lines, the male fish jumped high in the air beside the boat to see where the female was. He
(45) was beautiful and he had stayed. (*Pause.*) And the old man said, "That is the saddest thing I ever saw." (*Pause.*) So you see, he is more than a great fisherman. (*Silence.*)

(50) MARY: How long did the male stay?

MANOLO: Until she was butchered. We live this way. (*He rises.*) I must go.

TOM: Is there anything we can do?

MANOLO: No. He will come back. (*He
(55) leaves.*)

From *The Old Man and the Sea*, a teleplay by Roger O. Hirson based on the novel by Ernest Hemingway.

gaffed: speared, stabbed

21. Where is this part of the play set?

22. Mary's response, *Do I?*, in Line 11 suggests that she
    (1) fears she and Tom are drifting apart
    (2) has a biting sense of humor
    (3) no longer loves Tom

23. From the stage directions in Lines 11–12, you learn that Tom
    (1) is out of breath and needs to rest
    (2) is surprised and disappointed by Mary's doubt that he loves her
    (3) tries to get away from Mary after he sees how she looks

24. When Tom asks if the old man is his friend, Manolo
    (1) denies it
    (2) assures Tom that the old man is his friend
    (3) says that he and the old man have often fished together

25. When Manolo says that the old man is more than a great fisherman (Lines 29–30), he probably means that the old man is
    (1) his best friend
    (2) capable of great brutality
    (3) sensitive and deeply touched by things

Questions 26 to 30 refer to the following passage from a historian's lecture, which was later printed as an essay. Do not be put off by the first two words. They are Latin, and the author defines them.

Homo ludens, man at play, is surely as significant a figure as man at war or at work. In human activity the invention of the ball may be said to
(5) rank with the invention of the wheel. Imagine America without baseball, Europe without soccer, England without cricket, the Italians without bocci, China without Ping-Pong, and
(10) tennis for no one. Even stern John Calvin, the **exemplar** of Puritan self-denial, was once discovered playing bowls on Sunday, and in 1611 an English supply ship arriving at
(15) Jamestown found the starving

colonists suppressing their misery in the same game. Cornhuskings, logrollings, barn-raisings, horseraces, and wrestling and boxing matches have (20) engaged America as, somewhat more passively, the armchair watching of football and basketball does today.

Play was invented for diversion, exertion, and escape from routine (25) cares. In colonial New York, sleighing parties preceded by fiddlers on horseback drove out to country inns, where, according to a participant, "we danced, sang, romped, ate and drank (30) and kicked away care from morning to night." John Audubon, present at a barbecue and dance on the Kentucky frontier, wrote, "Every countenance beamed with joy, every heart leaped (35) with gladness . . . care and sorrow were flung to the winds."

Play has its underside, too, in the gladiatorial games, in cockfights and prizefights, which arouse one of the (40) least agreeable of human characteristics, pleasure in blood and brutality, but in relation to play as a whole, this is minor.

From "Mankind's Better Moments" by Barbara Tuchman.

exemplar: model

26. It is the author's opinion that
    (1) for human activity, the ball and the wheel are equally important inventions
    (2) John Calvin played bowls
    (3) John Audubon attended a barbecue and dance in Kentucky

27. Which of the following sentences from the passage best expresses its main idea?
    (1) In human activity the invention of the ball may be said to rank with the invention of the wheel.
    (2) Play was invented for diversion, exertion, and escape from routine cares.
    (3) Play has its underside, too.

28. The author's purpose in the passage seems to be to
    (1) entertain her readers with quotes about play from famous people
    (2) convince her readers to play more than they do
    (3) explain the importance of play in human life

29. The author probably thinks that fighting in a war
    (1) has been easier since the invention of the ball
    (2) is a kind of play
    (3) can bring out the most disagreeable human characteristics

30. Which of the following conclusions can you draw about the author's attitude toward play?
    (1) Play is more important for human beings than work.
    (2) Play serves mostly as a positive escape from regular concerns.
    (3) Play brings out people's pleasure in brutality.

Check your answers on page 189.

INTERPRETING LITERATURE AND THE ARTS READINGS 3
SKILLS CHART

To review the reading skills covered by the questions in Interpreting Literature and the Arts Readings 3, study the following parts of Units 1, 2, and 3.

Unit 1 Comprehending What You Read   **Item Number**

Chapter 1	Finding Details	1
Chapter 2	Finding Topics and Main Ideas	27
Chapter 3	Reading Dialogue	24

Unit 2 Inferring As You Read

Chapter 1	Inferring Unstated Details	8, 17
Chapter 2	Inferring Ideas and Drawing Conclusions	4, 7, 11, 19, 25, 30

Unit 3 Reading Critically

Chapter 1	Applying What You Read	
Lesson 12	Applying Ideas from Passages	5, 15, 29
Lesson 13	Applying Knowledge about Characters	10
Chapter 2	Analyzing What You Read	
Lesson 14	The Author's Purpose	13, 28
Lesson 15	Facts and Opinions	3, 12, 26
Lesson 16	Characterization	2, 22
Lesson 17	Setting	6, 21
Lesson 18	Mood and Tone	9, 14, 20
Lesson 19	Analyzing Drama	23
Lesson 20	Analyzing Poetry	16, 18

INTERPRETING LITERATURE AND THE ARTS READINGS 3
CONTENT CHART

The following chart shows the type of reading passage each item in
Interpreting Literature and the Arts Readings 3 refers to.

Type of Literature	Item Number
Nonfiction	1, 2, 3, 4, 5, 26, 27, 28, 29, 30
Fiction	6, 7, 8, 9, 10
Drama	21, 22, 23, 24, 25
Poetry	16, 17, 18, 19, 20
Commentary	11, 12, 13, 14, 15

This section will give you more practice at answering questions like those on the GED. As you do this Practice, use the reading skills you've studied in this book.

Directions: Choose the one best answer to each item.

Items 1 to 6 refer to the following passage.

WHO IS THE NARRATOR OF THIS PASSAGE?

This is my Man. I am not afraid of him. He is very strong, for he eats a great deal; he is an Eater of All Things. What are you eating? Give me some!

(5) He is not beautiful, for he has no fur. Not having enough saliva, he has to wash himself with water. He meows in a harsh voice and a great deal more than necessary. Sometimes in his sleep he
(10) purrs.

Let me out!

I don't know how he has made himself Master; perhaps he has eaten something sublime.

(15) He keeps my rooms clean for me.

In his paws he carries a sharp black claw and he scratches with it on white sheets of paper. That is the only game he plays. He sleeps at night instead of by
(20) day, he cannot see in the dark, he has no pleasures. He never thinks of blood, never dreams of hunting or fighting; he never sings songs of love.

From Toward the Radical Center: A Karel Capek Reader,
edited by Peter Kussi.

1. The passage is written as though the narrator were a
   (1) cat
   (2) professional writer
   (3) house cleaner
   (4) cook
   (5) woman

2. The sharp black claw in Lines 16–17 is probably a
   (1) finger
   (2) pen
   (3) fingernail
   (4) knife
   (5) hammer

3. The narrator characterizes the man as
   (1) strange
   (2) beautiful
   (3) quiet
   (4) ordinary
   (5) exciting

4. The tone of the passage is
   (1) serious
   (2) depressed
   (3) humorous
   (4) hopeful
   (5) angry

5. Which of the following pieces of advice might the narrator give the man?
   (1) Eat less.
   (2) Bathe more often.
   (3) Talk more.
   (4) Enjoy life more.
   (5) Work harder.

6. The author's purpose in writing this passage was probably to
   (1) convince readers that animals are superior to people
   (2) prove that people are superior to animals
   (3) explain the difference between the animal world and the human world
   (4) entertain the reader by writing from the point of view of an animal
   (5) portray the life of a lonely person

Items 7 to 10 refer to the following paragraph.

WHAT IS BASEBALL TIME?

Within the ball park, time moves
differently, marked by no clock except
the events of the game. This is the
unique, unchangeable feature of
(5) baseball, and perhaps explains why this
sport, for all the enormous changes it has
undergone in the past decade or two,
remains somehow rustic, unviolent, and
introspective. Baseball's time is
(10) seamless and invisible, a bubble within
which players move at exactly the same
pace and rhythms as all their
predecessors. This is the way the game
was played in our youth and in our
(15) fathers' youth, and even back then—back
in the country days—there must have
been the same feeling that time could be
stopped. Since baseball time is
measured only in outs, all you have to do
(20) is succeed utterly; keep hitting, keep the
rally alive, and you have defeated time.
You remain forever young. Sitting in the
stands, we sense this, if only dimly. The
players below us—Mays, DiMaggio, Ruth,
(25) Snodgrass—swim and blur in memory,
the ball floats over to Terry Turner, and
the end of this game may never come.

From The Summer Game by Roger Angell.

7. The topic of the paragraph is
   (1) time
   (2) ancestors
   (3) change
   (4) staying young
   (5) baseball

8. The word predecessors in Line 13
   refers to
   (1) all players
   (2) current players
   (3) previous players
   (4) future players
   (5) dead players

9. The main idea of the paragraph is that
   (1) within a ballpark, time is measured
       differently
   (2) you can defeat time by succeeding at
       baseball
   (3) you can remain forever young if you
       are a baseball player
   (4) baseball time is measured in outs
   (5) some baseball games seem to last
       forever

10. Which of the following conclusions can
    you draw from the paragraph?
    (1) Baseball, like most sports, is getting
        more violent.
    (2) If a baseball fan from the 1920s could
        see a game today, he would
        recognize the game.
    (3) In a baseball park a spectator gets a
        strong sense of the passing of time.
    (4) More than most sports, baseball is
        getting commercial.
    (5) Baseball is a completely different
        game from what it used to be.

Items 11 and 12 refer to the following poem.

WHAT CHARACTERIZES EACH AGE OF MAN?

THE FOUR AGES OF MAN
He with body waged a fight,
But body won; it walks upright.

Then he struggled with the heart;
Innocence and peace depart.

(5) Then he struggled with the mind;
His proud heart he left behind.

Now his wars on God begin;
At stroke of midnight God shall win.

By William Butler Yeats.

11. Each stanza describes a different
    (1) stage in an individual's life
    (2) century
    (3) human relationship
    (4) period of history
    (5) man

12. The poet sees each age of man as a kind of
    (1) puzzle
    (2) surprise
    (3) gift
    (4) battle
    (5) responsibility

Check your answers on page 191.

GED PRACTICE 3 SKILLS CHART

To review the reading skills covered by the items in GED Practice 3, study the following parts of this book.

Unit 1 Comprehending What You Read	Item Number
Chapter 2 Finding Topics and Main Ideas	7

Unit 2 Inferring As You Read

Chapter 1 Inferring Unstated Details	2, 8
Chapter 2 Inferring Ideas and Drawing Conclusions	1, 9, 10, 12

Unit 3 Reading Critically

Chapter 1 Applying What You Read	
Lesson 13 Applying Knowledge about Characters	5

Chapter 2 Analyzing What You Read	
Lesson 14 The Author's Purpose	6
Lesson 16 Characterization	3
Lesson 18 Mood and Tone	4
Lesson 20 Analyzing Poetry	11

GED PRACTICE 3 CONTENT CHART

The following chart shows the type of reading passage each item in GED Practice 3 refers to.

Type of Literature	Item Number
Nonfiction	7, 8, 9, 10
Fiction	1, 2, 3, 4, 5, 6
Poetry	11, 12

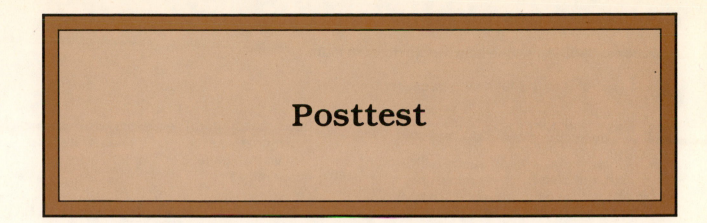

Posttest

The following Posttest is similar to the Interpreting Literature and the Arts Test of the GED. Taking it will help you find out how your skills have improved by using this book. It can also help you find out what you need to review or learn more about.

The Posttest has 23 multiple-choice items—about half as many as there are on the GED. The questions test your understanding of the readings and your ability to think critically about them.

Andres Segovia seems to regard his guitar with the *attentive courtesy* described in the poem "The Guitarist Tunes Up" in the Posttest.

Directions: Choose the <u>one best answer</u> to each item.

<u>Items 1 to 5</u> refer to the following passage.

WHAT WAS THE PONY-RIDER'S JOB?

The pony-rider was usually a little bit of a man, full of spirit and endurance. It didn't matter what time of the day or night his turn came. It didn't matter
(5) whether it was winter or summer, raining, snowing, hailing, or sleeting. It didn't matter whether he had a level, straight road or a crazy trail over mountains. It didn't matter whether it led through
(10) peaceful regions or regions with many dangers. He must be always ready to leap into the saddle and be off like the wind!

There was no idle time for a pony-rider on duty. He rode fifty miles without
(15) stopping, by daylight, moonlight, starlight, or through the blackness of darkness. He rode a splendid horse that was born for a racer and fed and treated like a gentleman. The pony-rider kept the
(20) horse at his utmost speed for ten miles. Then he came crashing up to the station where two men stood holding a fresh, impatient steed. The transfer of rider and mailbag was made in the twinkling of an
(25) eye. Away flew the eager pair and were out of sight before the spectator could get hardly the ghost of a look.

Both rider and horse traveled light. The rider's dress was thin and fitted close. He
(30) wore a short, tight jacket and a snug cap without a brim. He tucked his pants into his boot tops like a race rider. He carried no arms. He carried nothing that was not absolutely necessary. Because postage
(35) was <u>five dollars a letter</u> very little foolish mail was carried. His bag had business letters in it mostly.

His horse was stripped of all unncessary weight, too. He wore a little wafer of a
(40) racing saddle and no visible blanket. He wore light shoes or none at all. The little flat mail pockets strapped under the rider's thighs could each hold about the thickness of a child's first reader. They
(45) held many an important business and

newspaper letter. These were written on paper nearly as airy and thin as a leaf. In that way, thickness and weight were economized.

From <u>Roughing It</u> by Mark Twain.

1. Which of the following sentences from the second paragraph expresses its main idea?
   (1) There was no idle time for a pony-rider on duty.
   (2) He rode fifty miles without stopping, by daylight, moonlight, starlight, or through the blackness of darkness.
   (3) He rode a splendid horse that was born for a racer and fed and treated like a gentleman.
   (4) The pony-rider kept the horse at his utmost speed for ten miles.
   (5) The transfer of rider and mailbag was made in the twinkling of an eye.

2. The author emphasizes the price of a letter in Line 35 in order to
   (1) show how easily people wasted their money
   (2) suggest how much a pony-rider was paid
   (3) prove that the service was a bargain
   (4) indicate that the value of a dollar has dropped
   (5) show why the service was used for only serious matters

3. The description of the pony-rider's size and dress would almost fit today's
   (1) mail carrier
   (2) postal clerk
   (3) jockey
   (4) truck driver
   (5) mounted policeman

4. The mood this passage creates is one of

 (1) total relaxation
 (2) great energy
 (3) sheer boredom
 (4) serious danger
 (5) bubbling happiness

5. A conclusion you can draw about the typical pony-rider is that he

 (1) was quick to ask for help
 (2) let nothing stop him from getting a job done
 (3) demanded top dollar for his work
 (4) thought mostly of his own comfort
 (5) considered safety first

Items 6 to 10 refer to the following paragraph.

WHAT KIND OF MAN IS THIS FATHER?

 Frenetic as they were, he preferred weekends to the Wednesday nights when they ate together. At first he thought it was shyness. Yet they talked easily,
(5) often about their work, theirs at school, his as a disc jockey. When he was not with the children he spent much time thinking about what they said to each other. And he saw that, in his eight years
(10) as a father, he had been attentive, respectful, amusing; he had taught and disciplined. But no: not now: when they were too loud in the car or they fought, he held onto his anger, his heart buffetted
(15) with it, and spoke calmly, as though to another man's children, for he was afraid that if he scolded as he had before, the day would be spoiled, they would not have the evening at home, the sleeping in
(20) the same house, to heal them; and they might not want to go with him next day or two nights from now or two days. During their eight and six years with him, he had shown them love, and made them laugh.
(25) But now he knew that he had remained a secret from them. What did they know about him? What did he know about
(30) them?

From "The Winter Father" by Andre Dubus.

6. Which of the following could serve as a title for this passage?

 (1) Weekends Alone
 (2) Shy Children
 (3) A Father's Thoughts
 (4) Children's Fights
 (5) Keeping Secrets

7. What is the father's job?

 (1) teacher
 (2) doctor
 (3) disc jockey
 (4) student
 (5) magician

8. The father probably had the thoughts described in the passage

 (1) when he was a child
 (2) before he was married
 (3) before his children were born
 (4) after he was divorced
 (5) after his children were grown up

9. The father speaks to the children as though to another man's children (Lines 15–16) because he

 (1) is always fair
 (2) is afraid they would not want to spend time with him
 (3) is afraid of children
 (4) thinks manners come first
 (5) knows his children do not like him

10. The father probably

 (1) tries to control everyone around him
 (2) takes life's challenges easily
 (3) puts his job first in his life
 (4) worries about the consequences of his actions
 (5) has trouble disciplining children

Items 11 to 14 refer to the following poem.

WHAT DOES THE POET COMPARE THE GUITAR TO?

THE GUITARIST TUNES UP

With what attentive courtesy he bent
Over his instrument;
Not as a lordly conqueror who could
Command both wire and wood,
(5) But as a man with a loved woman might,
Inquiring with delight
What slight essential things she had to say
Before they started, he and she, to play.

By Frances Cornford.

11. The poet describes the guitarist as

    (1) commanding
    (2) lordly
    (3) playful
    (4) conquering
    (5) courteous

12. The words <u>wire and wood</u> in Line 4 refer
    to

    (1) the weapons of a warrior
    (2) a carpenter's supplies
    (3) the possessions of a conqueror
    (4) the materials that make a guitar
    (5) the tools of a fencemaker

13. Which of the following best describes the
    main reason the word <u>play</u> is used in the
    last line?

    (1) It reminds the reader that the man
        and the woman are not serious.
    (2) It reminds the reader that the poem
        is about guitars.
    (3) It rhymes well with the word <u>say</u>.
    (4) It links the actions of a guitarist and
        his instrument to those of lovers.
    (5) It helps the poem to have a light tone.

14. Which comparison best describes the
    central theme of the poem?

    (1) A musician and his instrument are
        like a carpenter and his tools.
    (2) A guitarist and his instrument are
        like two lovers.
    (3) A performer and his instrument are
        like a soldier and his enemy.
    (4) A conqueror and his army are like a
        guitarist and his instrument.
    (5) A musician is like an interviewer.

Items 15 to 18 refer to the following
passage.

WAS PICASSO A BORN ARTIST?

Picasso could draw before he could
speak. At the age of ten he could draw
from plaster casts as well as any
provincial art teacher. Picasso's father
(5) was a provincial art teacher, and before
his son was fourteen, he gave him his
own palette and brushes and swore that
he would never paint again because his
son had out-mastered him. When he was
(10) just fourteen the boy took the entrance
examination to the senior department of
the Barcelona Art School. Normally one
month was allowed to complete the
necessary drawings. Picasso finished
(15) them all in a day. When he was sixteen
he was admitted with honours to the
Royal Academy of Madrid and there were
no more academic tests left for him to
take. Whilst still a young adolescent he
(20) had already taken over the professional
mantle of his father and exhausted the
pedagogic possibilities of his country.

From The Success and Failure of Picasso
by John Berger.

15. The <u>pedagogic possibilities</u> in Line 22
    refer to opportunities in

    (1) employment
    (2) art
    (3) travel
    (4) education
    (5) housing

16. Which of the following conclusions can
    be drawn from the information in the
    passage?

    (1) Picasso could draw better than any
        other artist alive at his time.
    (2) Picasso was less talented than his
        father.
    (3) The talented young Picasso was
        better than older artists because he
        had a fresher view of the world.
    (4) Art schools taught Picasso little.
    (5) Picasso's extraordinary talent could
        be observed even when he was very
        young.

17. Which of the following best tells the author's purpose in writing this passage?
   (1) to prove that Picasso was no genius
   (2) to illustrate how talented Picasso was
   (3) to argue that artists are more important than other people
   (4) to describe the art schools of Barcelona and Madrid
   (5) to analyze Picasso's relationship to his father

18. Which of the following statements from the paragraph expresses an opinion of the author's?
   (1) Picasso could draw before he could speak.
   (2) At the age of ten he could draw from plaster casts as well as any provincial art teacher.
   (3) Picasso's father was a provincial art teacher.
   (4) When he was just fourteen the boy took the entrance examination to the senior department of the Barcelona Art School.
   (5) Normally one month was allowed to complete the necessary drawings.

Items 19 to 23 refer to the following passage from a play.

HOW DOES LINDA TREAT WILLY?

A melody is heard, played upon a flute. . . .

LINDA: (Hearing WILLY outside the bedroom, calls with some trepidation) (5) Willy!
WILLY: It's all right. I came back.
LINDA: Why? What happened (Slight pause) Did something happen, Willy?
WILLY: No, nothing happened.
(10) LINDA: You didn't smash the car, did you?
WILLY: (With casual irritation) I said nothing happened. Didn't you hear me?
LINDA: Don't you feel well?
WILLY: I'm tired to the death. (The flute (15) has faded away. He sits on the bed beside her, a little numb) I couldn't make it. I just couldn't make it, Linda.

LINDA: (Very carefully, delicately) Where were you all day? You look terrible.
(20) WILLY: I got as far as a little above Yonkers. I stopped for a cup of coffee. Maybe it was the coffee.
LINDA: What?
WILLY: (After a pause) I suddenly couldn't (25) drive any more. The car kept going off onto the shoulder, y'know?
LINDA: (Helpfully) Oh. Maybe it was the steering again. I don't think Angelo knows the Studebaker.
(30) WILLY: No, it's me, it's me. Suddenly I realize I'm goin' sixty miles an hour and I don't remember the last five minutes. I'm—I can't seem to—keep my mind to it.
(35) LINDA: Maybe it's your glasses. You never went for your new glasses.
WILLY: No, I see everything. I came back ten miles an hour. It took me nearly four hours from Yonkers.
(40) LINDA: (Resigned) Well, you'll just have to take a rest, Willy, you can't continue this way.
WILLY: I just got back from Florida.
LINDA: But you didn't rest your mind. (45) Your mind is overactive, and the mind is what counts, dear.
WILLY: I'll start out in the morning. Maybe I'll feel better in the morning. (She is taking off his shoes) These goddam (50) arch supports are killing me.
LINDA: Take an aspirin. Should I get you an aspirin? It'll soothe you.

From Death of a Salesman by Arthur Miller.

19. In which part of the day is the passage most likely set?
   (1) in the early morning
   (2) in the late afternoon
   (3) around noon
   (4) in the afternoon
   (5) at night

20. From the first three speeches, you can infer that Linda
    (1) had expected Willy to come home earlier than he did
    (2) had been waiting for Willy to get home
    (3) had not known that Willy had gone anywhere
    (4) had not expected Willy to come home when he did
    (5) had expected Willy to come home an hour later than he did

21. Which of the following stage directions gives a clue to the way Willy feels?
    (1) Lines 7–8: (Slight pause)
    (2) Line 11: (With casual irritation)
    (3) Line 18: (Very carefully, delicately)
    (4) Line 27: (Helpfully)
    (5) Line 40: (Resigned)

22. The first time Linda acknowledges that there might be something wrong with Willy is when she says
    (1) Did something happen, Willy? (Line 8)
    (2) Don't you feel well? (Line 13)
    (3) Oh. Maybe it was the steering again. (Lines 27–28)
    (4) Maybe it's your glasses. (Line 35)
    (5) Well, you'll just have to take a rest, Willy, you can't continue this way. (Lines 40–42)

23. If a hungry, stray dog appeared at Linda's back door, she would probably
    (1) chase it away
    (2) feed it
    (3) kick it
    (4) kill it
    (5) ignore it

Check your answers on page 192.

POSTTEST SKILLS CHART

To review the reading skills covered by the questions in the Posttest, study the following parts of this book.

Unit 1 Comprehending What You Read		Item Number
Chapter 1	Finding Details	7, 11
Chapter 2	Finding Topics and Main Ideas	1, 6
Chapter 3	Reading Dialogue	22

Unit 2 Inferring As You Read		
Chapter 1	Inferring Unstated Details	12, 15, 20
Chapter 2	Inferring Ideas and Drawing Conclusions	5, 14, 16

Unit 3 Reading Critically		
Chapter 1	Applying What You Read	
Lesson 12	Applying Ideas from Passages	3
Lesson 13	Applying Knowledge about Characters	23
Chapter 2	Analyzing What You Read	
Lesson 14	The Author's Purpose	2, 17
Lesson 15	Facts and Opinions	18
Lesson 16	Characterization	9, 10
Lesson 17	Setting	8, 19
Lesson 18	Mood and Tone	4
Lesson 19	Analyzing Drama	21
Lesson 20	Analyzing Poetry	13

POSTTEST CONTENT CHART

The following chart shows the type of reading passage each item in the Posttest refers to.

Type of Literature	Item Number
Nonfiction	1, 2, 3, 4, 5
Fiction	6, 7, 8, 9, 10
Drama	19, 20, 21, 22, 23
Poetry	11, 12, 13, 14
Commentary	15, 16, 17, 18

ANSWERS AND EXPLANATIONS

In this section are the answers with explanations for the questions in this book's Pretest, Exercises, Literature Readings, GED Practices, and Posttest. The reading skill and the type of literature tested are indicated for all questions except those in Exercises.

PRETEST (page 1)

1. **(5)** The clues are that Harry wants *to move to the country* (Line 3); he wants *a simpler life* (Line 5); he wants *a change* (Line 11). (Inferring Ideas and Drawing Conclusions/Fiction)

2. **(3)** Harry's wish for change suggests that he is not happy with his life as it is. (Characterization/Fiction)

3. **(4)** Line 1 says that Harry has lived in San Francisco for the last three years. Therefore, he still lived there when the conversation took place. (Setting/Fiction)

4. **(1)** The woman says that she could live in the country again because she has experience at it. She probably knows that Harry hasn't lived in the country, as Line 1 says, and wonders whether he could adjust. (Inferring Unstated Details/Fiction)

5. **(4)** The word *bleak* (Line 10) and the feeling that the woman is always watching him suggest that Harry is anxious. The tone is certainly not peaceful or amused. The feeling is not as strong as anger or fright. (Mood and Tone/Fiction)

6. **(2)** Line 3 states this. (Finding Details/Poetry)

7. **(1)** In the first stanza the poet says that in the daytime, both mice and bats like to stay in the attics of old houses. (Analyzing Poetry)

8. **(5)** The fourth stanza says we are afraid of something. The last stanza tells what it is. The poet thinks something is *out of place/When mice with wings can wear a human face.* (Analyzing Poetry)

9. **(4)** The words *afraid* (Line 8) and *amiss* and *out of place* (Line 9) suggest that there is something disturbing about the bat. (Mood and Tone/Poetry)

10. **(2)** Auden said *that he would ask the young man why he wanted to write poetry* (Lines 2–3). (Finding Details/ Nonfiction)

11. **(4)** The author wants to point out what *a fundamental part of the poetic process* is. This is a characteristic poets must have. (The Author's Purpose/Nonfiction)

12. **(1)** What Auden says in Lines 6–7 shows that he thinks it is fundamental that a poet have an appreciation for words. Auden doesn't say that a poet needs to do any of the things listed in the other choices. (Inferring Ideas and Drawing Conclusions/Nonfiction)

13. **(4)** Since Auden thinks that a poet must appreciate words, of the people listed in the choices, he would probably think that the one who likes to read dictionaries might have a chance at becoming a poet. (Applying Ideas from Passages/Nonfiction)

14. **(5)** John talks about Timmy always being home from school (Line 7), and Timmy tells the *corny* story John once told him about fathers. From these clues, you can infer their relationship. (Inferring Unstated Details/Drama)

15. **(2)** In Lines 16–17 John apologizes to Timmy for underestimating him. What Timmy says in Lines 18–22 is a kind of apology for not having always thought well of his father. (Inferring Ideas and Drawing Conclusions/Drama)

16. **(4)** John has just mentioned Dr. Goldman in Lines 12 and 13. (Reading Dialogue/Drama)

17. **(2)** Since John and Timmy both laugh, they must be feeling pleasant. Choices (1) and (3) would not go with laughing; there is nothing to suggest that John and Timmy are feeling silly (Choice 4) or foolish (Choice 5). (Analyzing Drama)

18. **(4)** Since John voluntarily apologizes to Timmy for underestimating him, he is probably the sort of person who takes—rather than tries to avoid—responsibility for the things he does. (Applying Knowledge about Characters/Drama)

19. **(1)** The paragraph describes *Life's* circulation between 1936 and 1969 as an example of the way picture weeklies grew more popular and then declined in popularity. (Finding Topics and Main Ideas/Commentary)

20. **(1)** From your experience, you probably know that *Life* is a picture magazine. The words *magazine* and *magazines* are used in the passage. From these clues you can infer the correct answer. (Inferring Unstated Details/Commentary)

21. **(5)** The circulation in 1940 was 3 million, and the peak was 8 1/2 million, or nearly 9 million. This is three times the 1940 circulation. (Finding Details/Commentary)

22. **(5)** The other statements can be proved, so they are fact. Choice (5) is an opinion with which some people might disagree. (Facts and Opinions/Commentary)

23. **(1)** *Life* must have been popular when its circulation was up to 8 1/2 million magazines a week. (Inferring Ideas and Drawing Conclusions/Commentary)

UNIT 1—COMPREHENDING WHAT YOU READ

EXERCISE 1 (PAGE 12)

1. The car is **an old station wagon** (Line 1).

2. **A man, a woman, and two boys** are in the car (Lines 2–3).

3. The month is **July** (Line 3).

4. The temperature is **one hundred plus** (Line 3).

5. The people look **whipped** (Line 4).

6. **Clothes, suitcases, and boxes** are inside the car (Line 4).

7. **(2)** In the last sentence you learn that *that's all they had left after the bank in Minnesota took* everything else they owned.

8. The Hopis are **patient** and **clever** and not at all **desperate** (Line 2).

9. The Hopis have been on their land for **ten centuries** (Line 3).

10. The Hopis grow **blue corn, squash, onions, beans, peppers, melons, apricots,** and **peaches** (Lines 4–5).

11. **(1)** In Lines 5–7 the writer says that both Hopis and the bristlecone pine live in adverse conditions.

12. The Hopis live with **poor soil, drought, temperature extremes,** and **high winds** (Lines 7–8).

13. Milkman discovered that **one of his legs was shorter than the other.**

14. **False.** Line 5 says *he never told anybody about it.*

15. Milkman had shooting pains **when he played basketball** (Lines 16–17).

16. Milkman felt connected to **President Roosevelt** (Line 18).

17. Macon is **Milkman's father** (Line 22).

18. **(4)** In Line 30 you learn that Milkman shared Macon's love for good shoes.

19. **(2)** The last sentence says that Milkman *did try, as his father's employee, to do the work the way Macon wanted it done.*

EXERCISE 2 (PAGE 18)

1. The interview takes place in **Chicago** (Line 6).

2. His first job is as a **busboy** (Line 7).

3. **(1)** Line 12 says the immigrant worker sends money back to his home.

4. **(3)** Lines 13–14 say people send money orders.

5. **False.** Lines 20–21 say *He doesn't care about union scale.*

6. **(3)** In Lines 20–21, the narrator says that the young worker will *work incredible hours* and *doesn't care about conditions.*

7. The name of the village is **Oraibi** (Line 1).

8. In 1901 the village population was **more than 800** (Lines 4–5).

9. **(2)** In Line 7 the writer mentions the woman.

10. Tomas Garces was **a Franciscan father** (Line 9).

11. **(3)** Unlike now, there were no television antennas in 1776. (Lines 10–12).

12. **(1)** Lines 10–11 say the *Hopis permitted Tomas Garces to stay.* Therefore, they accepted him. Line 12 says they *refused his . . . god,* so they did not accept his beliefs.

13. The poet says it is **impossible to describe** (Line 4).

14. The traveler is **sitting in front of an inn, sipping wine** (Lines 6–7).

15. The narrator talks to **an old man** (Lines 12–13).

16. They talk about **work and crops** (Lines 12–13).

17. **(1)** The word *office* (Line 16) suggests a job or responsibility.

18. **(3)** In Lines 15–18 the narrator says he might come back to the place after he retires.

EXERCISE 3 (PAGE 26)

1. **(3)** The writer has just mentioned a *stretch of weather* during a Vermont winter.

2. **(1)** The writer says this in Line 6.

3. **(3)** In Lines 7–8 the writer says that *you can heat two or three rooms with wood stoves,* and in the last sentence he says *That's what most of us do.*

4. **(2)** The phrases *Vermont winter, twenty below every night, keeping warm, keep the thermostat up, long underwear,* and *heat two or three rooms* all suggest that the topic is keeping warm in Vermont. Choices (1) and (3) are details about the topic.

5. In Lines 2–3 the writer says that people ask her why she doesn't write about the **struggle for power** and **security** and about **love**.

6. **(2)** In the first paragraph the writer says that people ask her why she writes about food. This suggests that her craft is writing.

7. In Line 8 she mentions the basic needs: **food, security, love.**

8. **(2)** She mentions that she also writes about love and warmth and other people (Lines 10–13).

9. **(1)** The writer does not mention that she likes to cook, and she does not tell how she got started as a writer. She answers the question people ask her in Line 1.

10. **(1)** In the first sentence the writer says that in *good moments, I've been able to say what I needed to say in Spanish.*

11. Mrs. Gonzales is the **owner of the motel** where the writer and his friends stayed (Line 12).

12. **(1)** In Lines 14–15 the writer says that Mrs. Gonzales complained *about some excess of celebration on our part.*

13. **(3)** The writer wanted to apologize for the behavior of his group, so he must have felt ashamed.

14. **(3)** In Line 24 the writer says that Mrs. Gonzales looked both *impressed* and *surprised.* He does not say that she was amused.

15. **(3)** The topic is the author's one success with the Spanish language. Choice (1), which comes from Lines 5–6, describes something about the author, but it is not the topic of the passage. Choice (2), which comes from Lines 25–26, describes only his reaction to Mrs. Gonzales' surprise.

EXERCISE 4 (PAGE 32)

1. **(3)** In Line 1 the narrator calls the blind man *an old friend of my wife's.*

2. **False.** He says that he *wasn't enthusiastic about* the visit (Line 8).

3. His idea came **from the movies** (Lines 9–10).

4. **(4)** In Line 8 the narrator says he *wasn't enthusiastic* about the blind man's visit, and in Line 9 he says the man's *being blind bothered me.* These feelings express the narrator's anxiety about the visit. Choice (1) tells what is about to happen. Choice (2) tells the narrator's feelings. Choice (3) is simply an observation.

5. **(4)** In Line 7 the narrator says that he had *no use for most of* the machines.

6. **(3)** Line 17 says *I saw myself as a good machine.*

7. **(1)** In Line 10 the phrase *as my pulse slowed down* suggests that he is near the end of his life.

8. **(3)** In Lines 6–7 you learn only that Abel Melveny had no sheds to put his tools in and no use for the tools. In Lines 9–10 you learn that he is thinking more clearly about himself. Lines 17–18 express what he has learned about himself.

9. **(2)** In Lines 1–2 you learn that *He had to get rid of the dog.*

10. **(3)** Lines 4–5 say *The sooner the better.*

11. **(1)** Line 5 says *He felt relieved making the decision.*

12. **(2)** Line 10 mentions *laying off,* and Lines 12–13 mention *cutting back.*

13. **False.** Lines 15–16 say that *friendship . . . didn't mean a damn.*

14. **(2)** The passage is mainly about the fact that nothing was going right for Al lately. Choice (1) describes Al's reaction to his decision to get rid of the dog. Choice (3) describes one of Al's problems.

EXERCISE 5 (PAGE 38)

1. **(3)** The man was working on the doorway, as Line 3 says.

2. **The man working on the house** or *stripping siding* (Line 1) came to the sidewalk and asked the author a question.

3. **(3)** *Careful work* was *done* with these objects (Line 15), so you can assume they are tools.

4. The man's name, **Bob Andriot,** is mentioned in Lines 15–16.

5. Andriot answers **ten days** (Line 18) when asked how long he had been at it.

6. **The author** asks the question after Andriot tells him when they want to move in.

7. Andriot mentions the **shape of the house** and **the low windows** in Line 23.

8. **Sydney's wife**, identified as *she*, first mentions a shed in Line 3.

9. (2) Sydney's wife refers to hydrangeas and dahlias as *Northern flowers* in Line 9.

10. (2) *He* is the man Sydney and his wife are talking about, the man they work for.

11. **Sydney** says this.

12. **Sydney's wife** says this. Notice that Sydney is identified as the speaker in the paragraph that follows.

13. (1) Sydney's wife wants *to know if it's permanent* (Lines 20–21). She worries that *he might pack up any minute and trot off someplace else* (Lines 21–22).

14. **Hammond** is first mentioned in Line 1, and **Hattie** is first mentioned in Line 7.

15. **Hattie** speaks first. She is talking to Hammond and addresses him by name in Line 1.

16. In Lines 1–4 Hattie asks twice for the **sugar** she sent Hammond to buy.

17. In Line 8 Hammond says that he **gambled that dime away.**

18. (2) In Lines 11–12 Hammond says that if Hattie is *a wise woman*, she *ain't gonna have nothing to say.*

19. **Hattie** says this. She has addressed Hammond by his name in the line before.

20. (1) In Line 17 Hammond says *I don't treat you bad.* Then in Lines 19–20 he says that he could treat her worse.

EXERCISE 6 (PAGE 43)

1. From the stage directions in Line 2, you learn that **it is raining.**

2. **Dodge** says this in Line 4.

3. **Halie** explains that Tilden is in the kitchen in Line 9.

4. (2) You learn in the introduction that Halie is not in the room with Dodge.

5. **Felix** says this in the first line.

6. In Line 4 Felix says that he can **cook.**

7. In Line 13 Felix says that Frances has his **big pot.**

8. You learn that **Oscar** picks up the phone in Line 15.

9. In Line 16 Oscar says hello to **Frances**.

10. **Oscar tells Felix** in Line 43 that Frances has just said that she wants Felix to pick up his clothes.

INTERPRETING LITERATURE AND THE ARTS
READINGS 1 (page 46)

1. **David** is first mentioned in Line 2, and his wife **Jessie** is also mentioned in Line 2. (Finding Details/Fiction)

2. **Jessie** says this. (Reading Dialogue/Fiction)

3. (1) Jessie says *your father* to David in Line 5. In the rest of the passage David and Jessie talk about his father. Each *he* and *him*, starting in Line 6, refers to the father. (Finding Details/Fiction)

4. (2) Choice (1) appears in Line 16. Choice (3) appears in Lines 28–29. In fact, the father does the opposite of Choice (2). He gives his food to other people (Lines 24–26). (Finding Details/Fiction)

5. **David** says this. (Reading Dialogue/Fiction)

6. (3) Jessie says this in Line 31. (Finding Details/Fiction)

7. (2) In Lines 1–3 the writer says that *her music* is *what will live on.* (Finding Details/Commentary)

8. (3) The writer refers to *graveyard quarrels as to who paid for her tombstone* (Lines 5–7). (Finding Details/Commentary)

9. **(2)** The word *pathos* (Line 26) suggests how sadly she spoke in Lines 24–25. (Finding Details/Commentary)

10. **(1)** The writer says *what will live on* (Lines 1–2) *needs no tombstone* (Line 7) and mentions *a monument to her* (Line 9). These phrases suggest preserving memories of Billie. The last paragraph is an account of one powerful memory the author had of Billie Holiday. (Finding Topics and Main Ideas/Commentary)

11. **(2)** Emma says this in Lines 6–7. (Reading Dialogue/Drama)

12. **(2)** Ella says *All we got is bacon and bread* (Lines 23–24). (Finding Details/Drama)

13. **False.** Ella appears not to know anything about the chicken. She says *Why would I use it?* (Line 27) and *Why should I use a fryer for soup* (Lines 29–30). (Finding Details/Drama)

14. **(3)** Ella says this in Lines 34–35. (Reading Dialogue/Drama)

15. The **rent man** speaks to Madam. He is identified in both the title and Line 1. (Finding Details/Poetry)

16. The **rent man** speaks first, in Line 2. He says *Howdy-do?* (Reading Dialogue/Poetry)

17. **Madam** says she will not pay the rent in Lines 8–10: *Before I'd pay/I'd go to Hades/And rot away!* She says it again in Lines 25–26: *If it's money you want/You're out of luck.* Both answers are acceptable. (Reading Dialogue/Poetry)

18. **(3)** Madam complains about the sink in Line 11, the window in Line 15, and the rats in Line 17. (Finding Details/Poetry)

19. **Madam** says this after the agent claims *I'm just the agent* (Line 21). (Reading Dialogue/Poetry)

20. **(2)** The topic is the argument about whether or not Madam is going to pay her rent. There is no evidence that the rent man is a stranger, and the descriptions of the broken things in the building are only a part of Madam's argument. (Finding Topics and Main Ideas/Poetry)

21. **(3)** She says this in the first sentence. (Finding Details/Nonfiction)

22. In Lines 10–11 she says that balance depends on the **individual.** (Finding Details/Nonfiction)

23. **(1)** The writer talks about places such as *military camps, schools,* and *prisons* (Lines 19–20) where many people must eat together. (Finding Details/Nonfiction)

24. **(2)** The writer says *Not all people need or want three meals each day* (Lines 5–6). This contradicts Choice (1). She also says that balance *depends entirely on the individual* (Lines 10–11). This idea suggests Choice (2) as a title. She gives no advice for Choice (3). (Finding Topics and Main Ideas/Nonfiction)

25. **(2)** Choice (1) supports the main idea by giving one of the author's opinions about balance. Choice (3) states a reality about large institutions. (Finding Topics and Main Ideas/Nonfiction)

GED PRACTICE 1 (page 51)

1. **(4)** The author says this in Lines 6–8. (Finding Details/Nonfiction)

2. **(5)** The author says *as though he were a knife-thrower* in Lines 15–16. (Finding Details/Nonfiction)

3. **(1)** The author says *I was enchanted* in Line 18. (Finding Details/Nonfiction)

4. **(5)** Choice (1) serves as an introduction to the passage. Choice (5) actually makes the comparison between news and fiction and noise and melody. Choice (2) is simply a side comment of the author's. Choices (3) and (4) are about his experience of melody. (Finding Topics and Main Ideas/Nonfiction)

5. **(3)** Walter says this in Lines 6–7. (Finding Details/Drama)

6. **(2)** Walter says this in Lines 17–18. (Reading Dialogue/Drama)

7. **(4)** Walter says this to explain what he thought he wanted for himself (Lines 2–3). (Finding Details/Drama)

8. **(2)** The author says that Ondine was *frightened that her heavy legs and swollen ankles will sink her* (Lines 6–7). (Finding Details/Fiction)

9. **(4)** The author says this in Lines 8–9. (Finding Details/Fiction)

10. **(4)** In the first part of the paragraph (Lines 5–10) the author describes Ondine's dreams. In the rest of the paragraph she describes Sydney's dreams. (Finding Topics and Main Ideas/Fiction)

UNIT 2   INFERRING AS YOU READ

EXERCISE 7 (PAGE 58)

1. In Lines 1–3 you learn that the mother read **ads, menus, billboards,** and **letters.** You could have answered any three of these.

2. You can infer that the narrator's name is **James.** The letter was in the narrator's drawer (Line 3), and the mother thought *James* had *nothing to hide* (Lines 4–5). These details imply that James is the narrator.

3. **(2)** Nothing suggests that the woman is crazy, and she doesn't seem to be looking for anything. Her actions are those of someone who is upset.

4. **(3)** According to the last sentence, the mother goes to mass *no matter how angry and confused she might be.* You can infer that she was angry and confused and upset from reading James's letter.

5. **Jim couldn't afford laundering** and **didn't believe in it,** according to Lines 3–4.

6. **(1)** Jim spoons baby food to Joel (Line 6). This implies that Joel is a baby—probably Jim's.

7. **(3)** Elbows and knees are often noticeable on tall, thin people—usually not short, fat people. Nothing in the phrase suggests mean or selfish.

8. **(2)** The author calls the arms of the chair *richly unsanitary* (Lines 10–11). The floor below the chair was probably even less sanitary. You can infer that the author hoped Jim would not feed the baby food that had fallen onto a dirty floor.

9. **(3)** In Line 2 the writer mentions *my mother.* In Lines 10–11 he mentions *the lady* and *her little boy.* These suggest a woman and her son.

10. The author says that they were driving to Utah **to get away from a man** (Lines 1–2) and **to get rich on uranium** (Line 2).

11. **(2)** The phrase suggests storms. Also, in Line 4 you learn that they left Florida *in the dead of summer,* which is a time of electrical storms.

12. **(1)** The phrase is used to describe the way people *spoke* (Line 9). As the woman and boy drove through different states, they heard different accents or ways of speaking.

13. **(1)** A *shortcut* is an easy way to get somewhere. Since she was driving, the woman probably asked for directions.

EXERCISE 8 (PAGE 63)

1. **(3)** Questions 2, 4, and 5 will help you discover the details that support this inference.

2. The narrator is sick of **rouging her cheeks.** This detail supports the inference required by Question 1.

3. According to Line 3, the face in the mirror **disgusts** the narrator.

4. **(1)** These are activities of a woman preparing for the day, not usually the activities of a man or a child.

5. The words suggest that the narrator is **old.** These words can describe a young person, but more often they fit someone who is old and tired.

6. You can infer that the narrator works **in a restaurant.** Some of the details from Questions 8 and 9 support this inference.

7. You can infer that the narrator's job is **waiting tables.** Some of the details from Question 8 support this inference.

8. The words **my station, my other tables,** and **menu** all suggest that the narrator is a waiter or waitress.

9. **(3)** As he gives his meal order, the fat man often says *we* rather than *I* when he talks about himself (Lines 17, 21, and 23).

10. **(2)** In Line 8 the narrator says *But it is the fingers I remember best.*

11. **(3)** In Lines 11–13 you learn that James P. Johnson had heard Morton in New York in 1911. The writer says, in Lines 15–16, that *Morton may well have been playing some sort of jazz in 1902.*

12. **(2)** The author describes Morton's claim in Lines 4–6.

13. **(1)** The author says that *Morton was a famous braggart* (Line 7).

14. **(3)** The writer gives evidence (Lines 13–16) that Morton did play something like jazz early in the century.

15. **(2)** The writer gives no evidence of this. He does support Choice (1) in Lines 19–20 where he says that *jazz pianists . . . did help to invent jazz.* He supports Choice (3) in Lines 15–18 where he says musicians were playing music *akin to jazz* in Harlem in 1902.

EXERCISE 9 (PAGE 68)

1. **(3)** This is the author's point in Lines 2–5.

2. **(1)** The two feelings contradict each other. One is positive—you try to be more generous. The other is negative—you get more angry and less generous.

3. **(1)** In Line 3 the writer gives his uncle's two nicknames.

4. **(3)** Since the writer has been talking about the way his father spoke, you can infer that the word has to do with speaking or talking.

5. **(2)** Milkman knew that he could never be like Macon, who seemed to be perfect.

6. **(2)** The answer is given in Lines 1–2.

7. **(3)** All the conditions described in Lines 2–3 are difficult, not comfortable or warlike.

8. **(2)** The writer had to protect his territory in the back seat against his sister's invasions.

9. **(3)** The writer and Sukey felt they had to protect their territories.

10. **(3)** In Lines 4–5 the poet says that life, or the hound, comes *Either to rend me/Or to befriend me.*

11. **(1)** The poet says that he doesn't know *The hound's intent/Till he has sprung/At my bare hand* (Lines 7–9).

12. **(2)** The poet has talked about not knowing, until the last moment, what life, or the hound, will bring.

EXERCISE 10 (PAGE 74)

1. **(2)** The words *he, him,* and *his* throughout the passage refer to the writer's friend, the painter in Scotland.

2. **(3)** The word *uncomprehending* (Line 4) suggests the writer's surprise or amazement when he looks at his friend who had *much the same origins* (Lines 4–5) as the writer. Nothing in the description expresses either pity or embarrassment.

3. **(3)** The author goes on to say that he came to *rest in a whole slew of places, countries, and languages* (Line 9). These details suggest living outside his original country.

4. **(1)** This is another suggestion that the author is different from or the opposite of his *rooted friend* (Line 10).

5. **(1)** In the last sentence the author says that the *peace with place* that his friend has made is *now beyond* the author.

6. (2) Much of the paragraph is about how opposite the two friends are. While the friend has lived his entire life in one town, the author has traveled a lot.

7. (1) The friend says that the cows *learned their lesson the first few days* (Line 6). The cows think that the wire is still "live."

8. (2) In Lines 8–9 the author mentions the *wire that no longer has the power to confine them*. This suggests that to be in bondage is to be confined, to be without freedom.

9. (1) Throughout the passage the writer mentions the words *fence* and *strand of wire*. At first the fence (Lines 1 and 5) is one that holds in two cows. Later the wire (Line 11) refers to restrictions on people.

10. (2) At the end of the passage, the author urges cows and people to *take your liberty* (Line 10). What we think holds us back may not be something that has any real power to confine us, just as the electric fence has no power.

11. (2) Since the child in the passage is identified as the woman's grandson (Lines 4 and 16), you can infer that *she* is a grandmother.

12. (3) The narrator punishes the little boy for hitting the grandmother. This suggests that the narrator is a parent of the little boy. The narrator *may* be the grandmother's child.

13. (1) The first sentence describes the woman remembering her childhood. In Lines 3–4 the author says that she can't *dice an onion, set the table,* or *play cards.*

14. (2) In Line 7 the boy *hits her because she can't remember anything.*

15. (1) Although the woman remembers her childhood, much of the passage is about her loss of memory. The little boy *hits her because she can't remember anything.* At the end of the passage you learn that she cannot remember that the little boy is her grandson. She asks, *Who does he belong to?* (Line 15).

EXERCISE 11 (PAGE 80)

1. (2) Each sentence refers to either trains or cars.

2. (3) An appendage is a limb of the body, such as an arm or a leg. Lines 9–10 give a clue. The author writes that we may lose *the use of our legs* because of our dependency on cars.

3. (2) In Lines 6–7 the author says he doubts *whether any truly absorbing conversation ever took place in a car.*

4. (2) In Lines 5–6 the author says that one *might as easily sit on a sofa and imagine a passing landscape* as *travel by car.*

5. (1) In the first sentence you learn the author's attitude toward trains. He thinks they *are for meditation, for playing out long thought-processes.* He trusts them. In the rest of the paragraph he criticizes cars.

6. (1) In Line 6 the writer calls the blanket *their home.*

7. (3) The first sentence talks about *father-love* and *his children.* You can infer that Kathi and David are the father's children. The father's name is used in Line 22.

8. (2) The father wants to make a point to his children, who are children of divorced parents.

9. (2) *Both* refers to something Kathi has learned. The narrator says that Kathi's *eyes were too tender, too wise.* He wishes that she could have waited longer to learn to be so tender and so wise.

10. (4) In Lines 3–4 you learn that things are finally as the father had *yearned for them to be in winter.* In Lines 28–29 the narrator talks about winter and the sound of car *doors closing and closing.* The father and his children have found a home together only in the summer.

11. **(2)** In Amanda's first speech she reminds Tom of her suggestion that he invite *some nice young man from the warehouse.* In Line 10 Tom says *I've asked him to dinner.*

12. **(1)** In Line 25 Tom says *He's coming tomorrow.*

13. **(2)** In Line 30 Amanda says *Tomorrow gives me no time!* She goes on to talk about preparations, making a fuss, wanting *things nice,* polishing, washing. She seems to want to put on a good show, and she needs more time.

14. **(1)** In Lines 47–48 Amanda says *It's terrible, dreadful, disgraceful that poor little sister has never received a single gentlemen caller!* You can infer that Amanda is eager to introduce Tom's sister to a man.

15. **(3)** The sentence that begins in Line 47, *It's terrible, dreadful,* suggests how important Amanda thinks a visit from a gentleman caller is. Tom expresses his feelings in Line 45: *Mother, this boy is no one to make a fuss over!*

INTERPRETING LITERATURE AND THE ARTS
READINGS 2 (page 85)

1. **(2)** Line 22 states that Charlie Harris is Shane's grandfather. (Finding Details/Fiction)

2. **(2)** *Institutions of the world* include courts. Mr. Harris is the sort of man who is likely to trust a judge—a representative of an institution—more than his grandson. (Inferring Unstated Details/Fiction)

3. **(1)** Nothing in the passage suggests that Shane had a bad back or that he was paying particularly close attention to things around him. You learn that Shane thinks the arrest and trial were *a farce* (Line 33). Lines 16–17 say that *the whole affair was no big deal to Shane.* These are clues that Shane did not care about what was going on. (Inferring Unstated Details/Fiction)

4. **(3)** In Lines 12–14 you learn that since Shane broke the antenna, *the judge was not entirely wrong.* (Finding Details/Fiction)

5. **(1)** The phrase *no big deal to Shane* (Line 17) and his description of the legal procedure as *a farce* (Line 33) are clues that Shane neither respects the police and courts nor feels changed by his experience. Choice (2) contradicts the evidence in the passage. Choice (3) is true, but it is not the main purpose. (Inferring Ideas and Drawing Conclusions/Fiction)

6. **(1)** Every sentence is about the office building (Finding Topics and Main Ideas/Nonfiction)

7. **(2)** The word *turntable* in the next line suggests something that turns. (Inferring Unstated Details/Nonfiction)

8. **(3)** The writer does not mention air-conditioning. In Lines 24–30 he mentions the qualities in Choices (1), (2), and (4). (Finding Details/Nonfiction)

9. **(3)** Frosted doors are made of glass to allow natural light in. The writer suggests that these doors are no longer widely used by building designers, who don't care so much about natural light. Nothing in the passage suggests that it was cold in the building in winter. Since the building once *held the altitude record* (Lines 12–13), you can infer that the building must have had some modern qualities. (Inferring Unstated Details/Nonfiction)

10. **(1)** The word *sway* suggests movement. (Finding Details/Nonfiction)

11. **(1)** In the first sentence you learn that people like Rose make the narrator *imagine them as babies, as young children.* (Finding Details/Fiction)

12. **(3)** In Lines 12–14 the narrator says that *there*—in kindergartens, in schools—*they enter the world a second time.* (Finding Details/Fiction)

13. **(1)** In Lines 25–26 the narrator says *out of fear they side with bullies or teachers.* (Finding Details/Fiction)

14. **(3)** The narrator says that when children support bullies and teachers rather than a friend, they give up their loyalty to the friend (Lines 25–27). (Inferring Unstated Details/Fiction)

15. **(3)** In Lines 18–21 the writer suggests that *with few adult exceptions*, abuse is more often inflicted by children, but this is not the main idea of the passage. It is an observation. He gives going to school the importance of entering the world for a second time (Line 14), but this is also not the main idea. It is a judgment. The main idea is the change that children undergo from innocence to something else. The writer is interested in the development from babies or young children—flushed cheeks and bright eyes (Line 8)—to older children, many of whom are corrupted *without knowing it* (Lines 21–22). This process or transformation is the main idea. (Inferring Ideas and Drawing Conclusions/Fiction)

16. **(1)** Jim asked Laura whether they had a class together in school. Laura answers that it was Chorus (Line 20). From that you can infer that they first met in school chorus. (Inferring Unstated Details/Drama)

17. **(3)** In Lines 29–30 Laura explains why she was always late. (Finding Details/Drama)

18. **(2)** In Line 33 the playwright indicates that Laura winces as she recalls the clumping of her brace. This clue lets you know that she is referring to the sound of her brace. (Inferring Unstated Details/Drama)

19. **Jim** first mentions the nickname *Blue Roses* in Line 49. (Reading Dialogue/Drama)

20. **(3)** You can infer from Lines 61–71 that Laura's handicap made her self-conscious and uncomfortable with other people during her childhood. In Line 76 Laura admits that she could never overcome her shyness, and in Line 80 she is sorrowful when she admits that one must work out of being shy gradually. All of these things lead to the conclusion in Choice (3). (Inferring Ideas and Drawing Conclusions/Drama)

21. **(1)** Each verse has the word *lose, losing, lost,* or *loss.* (Finding Topics and Main Ideas/Poetry)

22. **(2)** To be filled with the intent to be lost is to be determined to be lost. (Finding Details/Poetry)

23. **(3)** Nothing in the verse suggests either war or natural disasters like earthquakes. The poet probably lost cities, realms, rivers, and continents because she moved. (Finding Topics and Main Ideas/Poetry)

24. **(2)** After saying she lost cities, the poet says she lost realms, rivers, and a continent. These are even bigger than cities. (Inferring Unstated Details/Poetry)

25. **(3)** The poet says that it is possible to adjust to the loss of minor possessions—like keys—and of major possessions—like loved ones—but she says nothing about the losses being equal. (Inferring Ideas and Drawing Conclusions/Poetry)

26. **(2)** Leaving abruptly is a clue that people didn't like what they saw. (Finding Details/Commentary)

27. **(3)** The artist says that the woman was not hostile (Line 17). He says that she was intelligent (Line 43). He says that *She really wanted to know* about his art (Line 15). From that, you can infer that the woman was puzzled. (Inferring Unstated Details/Commentary)

28. The artist discussed the word **ugly** with the middle-aged woman. He wanted to know *what she meant by 'ugly'* (Lines 18–19). (Finding Details/Commentary)

29. **(2)** In Lines 28–35 the artist says that a description of the way the woman was dressed *might sound very much like what she'd been saying*—that her dress was ugly because its materials had been put together arbitrarily. (Finding Details/Commentary)

30. **(2)** In the first paragraph, the artist is described as *friendly*, as *responsive*, and

as someone *who made earnest efforts to get to the bottom of [viewers'] complaints.* In the last sentence the artist explains that the woman *hadn't been able to look at the pictures until somebody helped her.* These are clues that he is a person who believes that with help people can find meaning in modern art. (Inferring Ideas and Drawing Conclusions/Commentary)

GED PRACTICE 2 (page 92)

1. **(3)** At the beginning of the passage, you learn that the narrator probably lives with his parents because he says *my father came home* (Line 1) and *we ate supper* (Line 8). In Line 20 the mother suggests that the narrator *could get a job.* Taken together, these clues suggest as the strongest possibility that the narrator is an unemployed teenager living at home. (Inferring Unstated Details/Fiction)

2. **(4)** This is suggested by the wife's comment in the last sentence. The husband probably had worked as a golf pro at the club mentioned in Lines 2–3. (Inferring Unstated Details/Fiction)

3. **(3)** When the mother heard that her husband had lost his job, she *did not get mad or seem upset* (Lines 5–6). She laughed with her husband about it (Line 7). She suggested that she could apply for a job as a substitute teacher (Lines 9–12). She expressed the belief that people would offer her husband work (Lines 12–15) and called the situation *an opportunity in disguise* (Lines 15–16). All of these actions suggest that the mother does not worry but looks on the positive side of things. She also seems to accept and adapt to change. There is no indication that she tries to control other people. (Inferring Ideas and Drawing Conclusions/Fiction)

4. **(2)** Much of the paragraph is about being old. In fact, an *octogenarian* is someone in his eighties. The title of the book from which the paragraph comes is a clue. (Inferring Unstated Details/Nonfiction)

5. **(1)** The writer states this in the first sentence. (Finding Details/Nonfiction)

6. **(4)** While the octogenarian sits back, he imagines youthful activity, such as a walk in the woods with hunting or fishing gear (Lines 9–11). It is when he *creaks to his feet, bending forward to keep his balance* (Lines 11–12) that he realizes he is old. (Inferring Ideas and Drawing Conclusions/Nonfiction)

7. **(2)** Most of the details about Gonzalo tell what he does or does not do with the mail. Lines 20–21 imply that he is supposed to deliver mail. (Inferring Unstated Details/Nonfiction)

8. **(5)** In Lines 21–23 the writer says that his house *is the farthest outpost of inhabited land,* and that Gonzalo's *bike could not climb to the ridge.* (Finding Details/Nonfiction)

9. **(4)** The passage does not suggest that Gonzalo burns packages, but it does mention the other choices in Lines 2–3 and 15–17. (Finding Details/Nonfiction)

10. **(4)** Most of the stories are about how unsuited Gonzalo is to be a mailman. The first sentence states that the author *cannot think of anybody less suited to his vocation than Gonzalo.* (Finding Topics and Main Ideas/Nonfiction)

UNIT 3   READING CRITICALLY

EXERCISE 12 (PAGE 99)

1. **(3)** In Line 2 the author says that men *think with their party.* He uses the word *swarm* to emphasize people's tendency to think with a group rather than individually.

2. **(2)** The author says people *feel with their party* (Lines 5–6), *are happy in their party's approval* (Line 6), and *where the party leads they will follow* (Lines 6–7). Choices (1) and (3) require more individual thinking than most voters exhibit according to the author.

3. **(1)** In Lines 4–5 the author talks about his father's anxiety about being late for a

train, but implies in Lines 5–7 that he himself is less worried about being late for trains. Those are clues to the meaning of *punctuality,* which the author has already implied in Lines 2–3 is not very valuable.

4. (1) The author had to *unlearn* his father's lesson about punctuality.

5. (1) Since the author learned that punctuality is not very valuable, you can infer that he would not be disturbed if his guest arrived late.

6. (3) In the second paragraph the author doubts the necessity of putting iodine on every scratch. Therefore, he would probably *not* take the child to the hospital. He also seems too concerned about children simply to tell one to leave him alone.

7. (2) Since the author learned to question his father's lessons about punctuality, you can infer that he would be happy if his child grew up to be the kind of person who questions ideas.

8. (3) In the first sentence the author says that, more and more, work is lacking in pleasure. Just as prisoners wish they could escape from prisons, workers in factories and offices want to escape because they get no pleasure from their work.

9. (2) Most of the passage is about the author's concern that few people find pleasure in work.

10. (2) Since a hobby is something one pursues for pleasure, the author would probably admire a person who could earn a living pursuing something he enjoyed.

EXERCISE 13 (PAGE 103)

1. (3) There is no indication that the narrator cannot speak English well. Also, Minnesota is not known for its unusual names, although it is known to have many people of Scandinavian heritage. The narrator notes in Line 2 that there were as many Swedes as Germans— probably his ancestry. Throughout the passage you learn that the narrator's view of the world is a narrow one. Anything unlike

what he is familiar with strikes him as most unusual. You can infer that he has never heard Swedish names before.

2. (3) There is no reason to think that people in such large cities as Minneapolis and Saint Paul would be at all familiar with the politicians in a small place like Zenith. To the narrator, however, Zenith is most important. The phrase *never even heard of our mayor* (Line 12) expresses the narrator's surprise. Nothing in the passage suggests hatred. The narrator has probably not traveled much. If he had, he might not have such a narrow outlook.

3. (2) Just as he talked in the passage about the strangeness of the names he encountered in Minnesota, the narrator would probably talk about the strangeness of foreign food. He does not seem hostile or small-minded enough to throw the food away or refuse to eat it.

4. (3) Lines 5–6 say *Living had got to be such a habit with him that he couldn't conceive of any other condition.*

5. (1) To admit that nothing would equal him shows pride, if not pure arrogance.

6. (1) In the last sentence, you learn that the general *was willing to sit on the stage in his uniform so that they could see him.* This is more evidence of his pride and a clue that he likes to be the center of attention. Choice (2) is wrong because Line 4 says he *didn't give two slaps for her graduation.* Choice (3) is wrong because the general thinks *a procession full of schoolteachers* would be *deadly* (Lines 15–16).

7. (3) The phrase in Line 3 indicates that Deeds would have little patience for the types described in Choices (1) and (2). "Just folks" sound like his type.

8. (2) The author says that Deeds *is not much of a reader* (Line 8).

9. (3) The passage Deeds reads, with phrases like *longing for the art of the painter* and *exquisite hues* (Lines 19–20), contains just the florid style that Deeds would find pretentious.

10. **(2)** Since Deeds wasn't much of a reader, he probably wouldn't join a reading club. Since he had little tolerance for pretense, he probably doesn't care for sportscars. He does read newspapers, though, as Lines 8–9 say.

11. **(2)** A tuxedo would show too much pretense for Deeds. He probably does, in fact, wear work shirts and jeans.

EXERCISE 14 (PAGE 110)

1. **(3)** The author mentions both Venice and Kansas City in the passage, but they are mentioned because of their markets. The word *food* does not appear in the paragraph.

2. **(2)** The introduction to the passage reminds you that Venice is a city of canals, so produce travels by boat. In Lines 9–10 the author notes that the lack of truck noise distinguishes the Venice market from others.

3. **(3)** The author likes the cheesecake so much that he would stand in line even if the makers were not so likeable as the couple from Yonkers. You can infer that his Latin teacher was not so likeable.

4. **(2)** Choice (1) covers only one observation of the author's. The author himself seems to prefer markets, Choice (3), but he is not trying to convince the readers. While telling of his enjoyment of markets, the author amuses the reader with the unusual comparison of Venice and Kansas City and with the equally unusual comparison of the baker to his Latin teacher.

5. **(2)** Nearly every sentence describes a feature of the Polo Grounds.

6. **(3)** The author thinks the sights and emotions will slip out of his memory. This suggests that they are unimportant, not powerful or useful.

7. **(1)** The work *plock* describes the sound of a line drive hitting a barrier.

8. **(2)** In Line 16 the author says that he mourns all the things he described. We mourn things that we miss because they are dead or forever lost. He feels

something like the opposite of Choice (1) when he says that the loss of the things he liked about the Polo Grounds *constitutes the death of still another neighborhood* (Lines 16–17). He says nothing about his notions of progress.

9. **(1)** Although the author clearly liked the Polo Grounds, he says nothing about the place being better than newer ball parks. He does entertain with vivid descriptions pulled from his memory.

10. **(2)** The author mentions history throughout the passage. She makes comparisons to sociology, a field that utilizes statistics, but the word *history* keeps reappearing in the passage.

11. **(3)** In Lines 21–22 the author says *Human beings are always and finally the subject of history.*

12. **(3)** The author calls man *the Unknowable Variable* (Line 21), and she says that *human beings* are the subject of history. Human beings are not always predictable. Their actions are not always logical. She does not argue that history is illogical because it is not a science (Choice 1). She also does not accuse sociologists of making history illogical (Choice 2).

13. **(1)** In Line 6 the author says that history cannot meet scientific standards. In the last paragraph she explains why. The author does not try to convince us that history is more important than science. Her purpose is to show that, because of the unpredictable nature of human beings, history cannot use the methods of science. The author has not included entertaining stories in the passage.

EXERCISE 15 (PAGE 116)

1. The statement can be accepted as **a fact.** You could prove it by seeing the movie yourself.

2. **(1)** In the first sentence, the reviewer says that *In the middle . . . the movie . . . Christy Brown . . . is in a restaurant.*

3. When Christy Brown paints, **he holds a brush between his toes.** (See Lines 4–5.)

4. **(1)** You could prove that this statement from the review is a fact by seeing the movie for yourself. Choices **(2)** and **(3)** could not be proved, so they are opinions. Some people might not have thought that the scene was fast or that the movie was not soft or maudlin.

5. **(2)** The words *owner's manuals*, *manual*, and *manuals* are used several times throughout the passage. The first two paragraphs are about owner's manuals in general; the last paragraph is about a particular manual.

6. The author's statement is **a fact.** Since cars were first built in the 19th century, there could not have been manuals for automobiles before then. In addition, you could prove that the first manuals appeared before the 20th century by looking at a manual written in the 19th century.

7. The statement is **an opinion.** There is no way to prove that prose, or writing, is dense—so that part of the statement is an opinion. It is also an opinion that the automobile manuals are of *little or no use.* Some people might find them quite useful.

8. You can take the statement for **a fact.** It would be possible to prove it by reading in the manual for Hardwick stoves, itself.

9. **(2)** In Lines 20–21, the author says that the manual *mostly upholds the old tradition.* In the first two paragraphs, the writer has explained how bad the tradition is.

10. The statement about the page numbering is **an opinion.** Some people might not find the page numbering confusing.

11. What the author says about the instructions is **a fact.** It would be possible to prove it by reading the Chevrolet owner's manual.

12. **(2)** In Line 3, the author says that *manuals have never been easy to read,* so Choice **(1)** is not correct. In Lines 9–10, he says that *most owner's manuals contain a great deal of surplus information,* and in Lines 30–31, he says

that an *owner . . . may be tempted to hurl the jack . . . through the . . . rear window.* These clues together allow you to infer that the author thinks manuals cause frustration. He does not suggest, however, that the manuals are impossible to use.

EXERCISE 16 (PAGE 121)

1. **(3)** See the second sentence.

2. **(2)** In Line 3 you learn that *Bailey was the son she [the grandmother] lived with.*

3. **(2)** Although the passage doesn't make it clear, you may infer that the young woman, who is described in Line 14 as *the children's mother,* is also Bailey's wife.

4. **(3)** The grandmother takes advantage of the story of The Misfit to argue her case for going to Tennessee.

5. **(2)** In the first two lines you learn the grandmother's intentions. She wants to persuade Bailey to take his family—including her—to Tennessee rather than to Florida because she wants to visit people there. She doesn't try to change an opinion Bailey holds, and she doesn't really have her grandchildren's welfare in mind. She wants what she wants, even though she tries to disguise that with clever arguments.

6. **(1)** See Line 2.

7. **(3)** See Line 4.

8. **(1)** In Lines 6–8 you learn that the daughters trip and drop things *under the frozen heat of [their father's] glance.*

9. **(2)** The last sentence means that the daughters have learned to live with the tension their father created and that they would not know how to live without it. Therefore, they are emotionally controlled by their father.

10. **(1)** The writer says that Macon was *likely to erupt* (Line 1), that he *kept each member of his family awkward with fear* (Lines 1–2). Therefore, he is not warm and supportive, and he probably has little sense of humor.

11. (1) Lines 9–10 say Reilly studied people *for signs of bad taste in dress.*

12. (1) From his cap to the potato chip crumbs to the baggy pants, Reilly's appearance seems strange, out of the ordinary, and unattractive.

13. (3) Anything new or expensive was an offense *against taste and decency,* according to Lines 11–12.

14. (2) See Lines 13–14.

15. (2) Throughout the passage you learn about both Reilly's unusual appearance and his exacting, if eccentric, demands about others and himself. He seems to not even want to blend in with others (Choice 1), and he certainly doesn't accept others easily (Choice 3).

EXERCISE 17 (PAGE 127)

1. Lionel and Ulysses explore **a library.** See Lines 11 and 13.

2. (2) To emphasize the silence of the building, the author uses the phrase *profound and almost frightening silence* (Line 2) and says *the walls had become speechless* (Line 3), and *silence had engulfed everything* (Line 4).

3. (3) It was not the hush in the library, nor consideration for the people who were trying to read there that made him whisper. As Lines 9–10 say, Lionel *whispered . . . out of respect for books.*

4. (1) In Line 12 the author says that the boys found many treasures, *Lionel—books, and Ulysses—people.* This suggests that Ulysses has an interest in people.

5. (2) Lionel thought people were quiet *out of respect for books* (Line 10). The author says that Lionel *just liked to see them—the thousands of them* (Line 14). In Lines 16–17, Lionel keeps repeating *these* and *all these.* He seems to be in awe of books, which shows great respect.

6. (3) There are several clues that the setting is a bustling seaport. In Lines 1–2 the *green sea* is mentioned. Line 4 mentions *a coast.* Line 5 mentions *the*

pier. Line 6 mentions *our ship.* These four clues, taken together, suggest a seaport. The *railway boxcars* in Line 5, the *hundreds of men* in Line 6, the *noise* in Line 9, and *the passport official* in Line 10 suggest the bustle of that seaport.

7. (3) Lines 6–7 say that the men didn't come *to welcome us but to quarrel with each other.* No mention of the men's heights is made in the passage.

8. As Line 9 says, the children were alarmed, or bothered, by **the heat and noise** in the setting.

9. (1) The busyness and quarreling did not make the port welcoming. The mother probably holds her breath because of the tension she feels. Nothing in the passage suggests bad smells or anything that would make it hard to breathe.

10. (2) The children did not *go on ahead,* as their father suggested in Line 8, because they were alarmed. Rather, they waited for him and *followed with Mother* (Line 11), who was *holding her breath* (Line 12). These actions suggest anxiety about the future, not enthusiasm or indifference.

11. (3) Lines 5–6 say the mother put a dime in the machine (the nickelodeon) and played music.

12. (2) In both Lines 5 and 13 the mother put a dime in the machine.

13. (1) The word *nickelodeon* is not used these days, and using a coin-operated record player costs more than 10 cents. These are clues that the passage is set in the past.

14. (1) As Lines 1–2 say, The Tower has *a counter* and *tables.* Lines 4–5 say that Red Sam's wife *took their order.* These clues suggest that The Tower is a restaurant.

15. (2) In Line 18 June Star calls The Tower *a broken-down place.* (Another indication that The Tower is rather run-down is the mention of the *board table* in Line 3.)

1. (3) In Lines 7–8 Adam says *Eden always had the disadvantage for me personally of being a little too lush and orderly.* He does not complain about thorns. In Lines 4–5 he says that he is used to them. In Lines 8–9 Adam says that he likes *some grit to my mash.* This is not a complaint about Eden's food.

2. (1) See Line 15.

3. (2) Adam does not seem sad or fearful as he begins to tell his story. Rather, he seems to look forward to telling it. But, since he doesn't seem to mind that it might cause some *embarrassment in Heaven* (Line 14), he could be considered a bit irreverent.

4. (3) Throughout the passage, Adam's tone is as informal as that of a person being interviewed on a television talk show.

5. (3) The main thing that makes this passage humorous is the language Adam uses. It sounds very informal and modern—quite unlike the language of the Bible from which the story comes.

6. (2) The waiter, first mentioned in Line 4, is a clue that the setting is a restaurant.

7. (3) Wayne is angry that the woman has said *There's always a chance* (Line 12). He continues *Answer me straight for a change* (Lines 13–14).

8. (1) Wayne has just expressed his impatience when he says *Don't give me that kind of crap* in Line 13.

9. (1) In Line 22 the woman says that she is *Thirty-seven tonight.* This is a clue that it is her birthday.

10. (3) Wayne's mood is bad throughout the passage. He first complains about the waiter and then shows his irritation with the woman, who seems unwilling to make a commitment to him. The woman is irritated in the middle of the passage.

11. (2) The first sentence mentions *the sounds of the rodeo around me.* In Line 3 you learn that the narrator is on a horse.

There is no mention of cowboys' work or horse training.

12. (2) These words suggest things that are wound up and about to jump. Such things are under great tension.

13. (1) The paragraph has many words about movement—*wheeling and spinning, tilting and beating, whirl, waving, pounding and leaping, turning,* etc. This paragraph recreates the movements of a rider on a wild horse.

14. (1) The paragraph uses mainly short sentences and phrases to describe a lot of fast, jerky movement. It creates in the reader a sense of excitement, not of sorrow or defeat.

15. (2) The rider is *on the ground, unmoving.* The rider's hands are *sunk in the dust of the arena.* You can infer that the rider has been thrown from the horse.

EXERCISE 19 (PAGE 139)

1. (3) The first stage direction says that the scene is set at Santiago's shack. Since he lives in a shack, he is probably rather poor.

2. (3) In Lines 9–11 you learn that Santiago feels lonely when he looks at the picture of the woman Angela calls Momma. You can infer that "Momma" is Santiago's wife and that she has died.

3. (3) In her speech that begins in Line 18, Angela explains that she wants her father to move into her and her husband's house in Havana.

4. (2) In Lines 41–44 Santiago imagines what his life in Havana with Angela might be like. He wants to continue to use his hands and arms. He seems to believe that his luck at fishing will change.

5. (2) The stage direction in Line 46 shows that Santiago is angry.

6. In Line 3 Timmy says that the bravest thing he did was that **he slept with his boots off when he was in combat;** in Line 15 he says that the smartest thing he did was that **he never volunteered.**

7. **(2)** In Lines 9–11 Timmy tells his dad that the guys who *cracked up* were the ones who didn't get enough sleep. He didn't want to be one of them, even though he must have known that taking his boots off in combat could be dangerous.

8. **(3)** In Lines 15–19 Timmy explained how he never volunteered to do anything. He tells his father *The fact is I wasn't a very good soldier* (Line 19).

9. When he says *You'd have been a good one*, Timmy expresses **an opinion**. What he says cannot be proved.

10. **(3)** Lines 30–31 say *When they learned I was the sole support of the family, they turned me down.*

11. **(1)** The stage directions in Lines 19–21 show that Troy and Rose have been talking on the porch outside a house. You can infer that it is their house.

12. **(3)** In Line 2 Rose tells Troy *I want you to act like my husband.*

13. **(2)** In Line 5 Rose accuses Troy: *You going down there to see her ain't you.* The *her* refers to Alberta, the woman Troy has been seeing.

14. **(3)** See Lines 14–15.

15. **(3)** Rose is sad that her marriage is in trouble and that Troy has received bad news. Troy is sad about Alberta's death.

EXERCISE 20 (PAGE 147)

1. The poem is divided into **four** stanzas.

2. The last word of the first line in each stanza rhymes with the last word in the **second** line. For example, *die* rhymes with *sky* in the last stanza.

3. **(1)** The poet says *For all they [the stars] care, I can go to hell.* Stars, of course, can neither care nor fail to care.

4. **(3)** The poet uses words like *indifference* (Line 3), *passion* (Line 6), and *affection* (Line 7), which usually apply to human relationships.

5. **(2)** The poet's subject is both stars and human relationships. He admits in the last stanza that although it might take him a little time, he could learn that *total dark* (the absence of stars and human relationships) can be *sublime*.

6. The last word in the first line of each stanza rhymes with the last word of the **third** line. For example, *knuckle* rhymes with *buckle* in the third stanza.

7. **(3)** The title is one clue. Lines 3–4 of the first stanza are another.

8. **(1)** The title, "My Papa's Waltz," is a clue. Another clue is that the narrator's ear is only as high as Papa's buckle.

9. **(2)** Nothing in the poem implies that the mother does not approve of dancing or that she was unfriendly. You can infer that the mother is worried about what is described in the poem—a father drunkenly dancing with his child.

10. **(1)** The child comes to the height of the father's belt and during the rough dancing scrapes an ear.

11. **(3)** The pans sliding from the shelf, the mother's frown, the scraping of the father's belt buckle, and the father's beating time on the child's head with a dirty hand are all things that probably frightened the child. The child's fondness shows in Lines 3 and 16 as he holds on to his father.

12. The poet says (a) his mistress' eyes are **not like the sun**; (b) her lips, **not like coral**; (c) her breasts, **not like snow**; (d) her cheeks, **not like damasked roses**; (e) her breath, **not like perfume**; and (f) her voice, **not like music.**

13. **(2)** The negative comparisons make the mistress seem quite ordinary.

14. **(2)** At the end the poet says his love for his mistress is *as rare/As any she belied with false compare.* Loosely reworded, this means that the poet's love for his mistress is as great as any love she may have felt from others.

15. **(3)** It is more common for a poem to celebrate rare beauty. This poem is humorous because it describes a woman who is not only not beautiful but is rather ordinary.

INTERPRETING LITERATURE AND THE ARTS
READINGS 3 (page 151)

1. **(2)** See the first sentence. (Finding Details/Nonfiction)

2. **(3)** The author says that Phoebe Hurty taught him *to be impolite . . . about American history and famous heroes, about the distribution of wealth, about school, about everything* (Lines 10–15), and he says that *she was funny* (Line 10). For the author she was *liberating* (Line 10). These are clues that he liked both her ideas and her style. (Characterization/ Nonfiction)

3. **(1)** The author says that Phoebe Hurty *was funny* (Line 10) and that her kind of *impoliteness is* now *fashionable* (Lines 32– 33). These are simply his opinions, with which other people could disagree. It can be proved as a fact, however, that, as a teenager, the author was required to wear the clothes he praised in writing. (Facts and Opinions/ Nonfiction)

4. **(1)** The author says that Phoebe Hurty taught him to be impolite about conventional ideas. This suggests that Phoebe Hurty encouraged him to ask questions and to doubt some of the truths he had been taught. (Inferring Ideas and Drawing Conclusions/ Nonfiction)

5. **(2)** Lines 10–15 show that Phoebe Hurty encouraged the author to think for himself. Lines 16–17 say that he now makes his living at it. Since he has found thinking for himself valuable in his own life, he probably thinks people in general, children included, should think for themselves, as well. Choices (1) and (3) suggest ideas opposite to that. (Applying Ideas from Passages/Nonfiction)

6. **(a)** Because it is snowing, it is **winter**. **(b)** Because it is dark and most of the stores are closed, it is **late evening** or **nighttime**. **(c)** Throughout most of the passage, Anna is **sitting in the front seat of a car, on the driver's side, parked in the lot of a shopping center**. (Setting/Fiction)

7. **(1)** Lines 18–20 say that Anna has begun to think that their plan was doomed, and Lines 30–32 show that Anna is afraid. Choice (2) is not correct because the knife was a toy only in Anna's imagination. Choice (3) says something that Anna believes, but it is not the author's main purpose in Lines 18–32 to show just that one thought of Anna's. (Inferring Ideas and Drawing Conclusions/Fiction)

8. **(2)** *A lot* (Line 43) refers to the money that Wayne got. In the first part of the passage, the author describes the way Anna would watch out in case a police cruiser came by, so Wayne must have been doing something illegal. (Inferring Unstated Details/Fiction)

9. **(2)** Anna's tension and fear are described in Lines 29–32. Wayne's running to the car and saying *Jesus Christ* three times as Anna drives away show his tension and fear. Anna and Wayne are in no way calm and relaxed (Choice 3). There doesn't seem to be secrecy and betrayal (Choice 1) because Anna and Wayne act as though they are in this together. (Mood and Tone/Fiction)

10. **(3)** In the passage Anna shows doubts about herself and the plan she has made with Wayne. That suggests a lack of self-confidence, which doesn't support Choice (1) but does support Choice (3). Anna's worrying in the passage shows that she is concerned about important things, so Choice (2) is not supported. (Applying Knowledge about Characters/ Fiction)

11. **(3)** The author says *the manual is prepared* for the readers' questions (Line 11) and that *it is readable* (Line 6). He ends the passage with examples of the manual's usefulness. (Inferring Ideas and Drawing Conclusions/Commentary)

12. (2) It would be possible, by looking at the manual, to see that each action shot has directions. Choices (1) and (3) are the author's opinions with which someone else could disagree. (Facts and Opinions/Commentary)

13. (1) The passage mentions good points about only the LeSabre manual, not automobile manuals in general, so Choice (1) is right and Choice (3) is wrong. The passage does not say anything about LeSabres, themselves, and doesn't try to convince anyone to buy one, so Choice (2) is wrong. (The Author's Purpose/Commentary)

14. (2) The tone of the passage is almost bouncy, as the following phrases and sentences illustrate: *strikingly different* (Line 2); *Better yet,* (Line 5); *Have to change a flat?* (Lines 6–7); *It expected that* (Lines 11–12). (Mood and Tone/Commentary)

15. (2) The author likes the pictures and the simplicity of the LeSabre manual. He would probably like an illustrated cookbook and a simple, illustrated First Aid booklet. Because federal income tax form directions are difficult to read and have few illustrations, the author would probably least like to read them. (Applying Ideas from Passages/Commentary)

16. (2) See Line 19. (Analyzing Poetry)

17. (3) The white coat and stethoscope (Line 19) are used by doctors. (Inferring Unstated Details/Poetry)

18. (3) See Lines 26–28. (Analyzing Poetry)

19. (1) The poem shows that the father is aging (Choice 2), but the main point is that with his aging comes the falling away of reserve, or emotional restraint, which the daughter loves. (See Lines 25–29, especially.) Choice 3 refers to Lines 18–23, which explain that the father was less open about his feelings when he was caught up in his work. (Inferring Ideas and Drawing Conclusions/Poetry)

20. (1) There is a sense of sorrow in the poem that the father is aging. There is also a sense of regret for the distance that once existed between the father and the author. But, mainly, the author describes her father with a good deal of fondness throughout the poem. (Mood and Tone/Poetry)

21. As the stage direction in Line 1 says, this part of the play is set on **Dune Road** near the beach. (Setting/Drama)

22. (1) In Line 9 Mary expresses that she feels left out of Tom's thoughts and plans. This is a clue that her unsure response to his saying that he loves her reflects worry about their relationship. Nothing suggests that she has a biting sense of humor (Choice 2) or that she is no longer in love (Choice 3). (Characterization/Drama)

23. (2) It is important to look at what Tom does in light of the conversation that comes before. He has reminded Mary that she knows he loves her (Line 10). When she asks *Do I?*, he stops and stares at her—probably with some surprise but with disappointment that she seems to have doubts. (Analyzing Drama)

24. (3) See Lines 23–24. (Reading Dialogue/Drama)

25. (3) The story about the male and female marlins illustrates this. (Inferring Ideas and Drawing Conclusions/Drama)

26. (1) It cannot be proved that the ball and the wheel are equally important inventions, but in Lines 3–5 the author says that she thinks they are. The statements about Calvin and Audubon can be proved to be facts, not opinions, by reference to eye-witness accounts. (Facts and Opinions/Nonfiction)

27. (2) As the first two words in the passage, *Homo ludens*, suggest, the whole passage is about what play means to people. The discussion about the ball (Choice 1) is only one aspect of play, just as the discussion about play's underside (Choice 3) is. (Finding Topics and Main Ideas/Nonfiction)

28. (3) The author's purpose is to explain. Her many examples and quotes from famous people are to make points clear, not to entertain the reader (Choice 1).

Nowhere does she try to convince people to play more (Choice 2). (The Author's Purpose/Nonfiction)

29. **(3)** In Lines 41–42 the author defines the most disagreeable human characteristics as *pleasure in blood and brutality.* Wars can bring out those characteristics. The author probably does not think that war is a kind of play (Choice 2) because in Lines 1–2 she distinguishes between man at play and man at war. Since she associates the ball with play, she probably would not see an important relationship between its invention and war (Choice 1). (Applying Ideas from Passages/Nonfiction)

30. **(2)** What the author says in Lines 23–25 supports this choice. Choice (1) is not correct because in Lines 1–3 the author says that man at play is as significant as man at work. Choice (3) is not correct because the author suggests that some play—not all play—brings out people's pleasure in brutality. (Inferring Ideas and Drawing Conclusions/Nonfiction)

GED PRACTICE 3 (page 159)

1. **(1)** The narrator says that the man *meows in a harsh voice* (Lines 7–8) and that he sometimes purrs in his sleep. These are the main clues that the narrator is a cat. (Inferring Ideas and Drawing Conclusions/Fiction)

2. **(2)** Since the man uses the claw to scratch *on white sheets of paper* (Lines 17–18), you can infer that it is a pen. (Inferring Unstated Details/Fiction)

3. **(1)** The cat-narrator characterizes the man as strange—not at all ordinary—because of the many ways he differs from a cat. The narrator does not describe the man as beautiful (see Line 5), quiet (see Lines 7–8), or exciting (see Lines 18–23). (Characterization/Fiction)

4. **(3)** The humor is in seeing ourselves through the eyes of a cat. (Mood and Tone/Fiction)

5. **(4)** The last paragraph, especially Lines 21–23, show that the cat-narrator thinks the man's life is rather boring because he doesn't enjoy any of the things a cat does. The narrator is not critical of the amount of food the man eats or of his bathing schedule. The narrator thinks the man already talks too much (see Lines 8–9), but doesn't mention work at all. (Applying Knowledge about Characters/Fiction)

6. **(4)** The author's purpose is probably to entertain. He makes no strong points about animals or people being superior. The differences he points out are only the most obvious ones. He has said nothing about the man feeling lonely. (The Author's Purpose/Fiction)

7. **(5)** The topic of the paragraph is baseball. The author talks about baseball as having its own kind of time. (Finding Topics and Main Ideas/Nonfiction)

8. **(3)** In Lines 13–15 the author says *This is the way the game was played in our youth and in our fathers' youth.* The players at those times came before today's players. (Inferring Unstated Details/Nonfiction)

9. **(1)** The whole passage explores how different the passing of time seems during a baseball game. (Inferring Ideas and Drawing Conclusions/Nonfiction)

10. **(2)** Because the pace and rhythms of the game haven't changed, a fan from the past would recognize the game today. Choice (1) is wrong because Line 8 says the game is still unviolent. Choice (3) is almost the opposite of the main idea. The author mentions nothing about commercialism and does not say that the game is completely different, even though there have been enormous changes. (Inferring Ideas and Drawing Conclusions/Nonfiction)

11. **(1)** The first stanza describes infancy. The second describes a loss of innocence. The third describes losing pride. And the fourth is about death. These are stages of life, as the poet sees it. (Analyzing Poetry)

12. **(4)** The first stanza mentions *a fight*. Stanzas 2 and 3 say a man *struggled*, and Stanza 4 mentions *wars*. (Inferring Ideas and Drawing Conclusions/Poetry)

POSTTEST (page 164)

1. **(1)** The whole paragraph explains why the pony-rider was never idle. The sentences in Choices (2), (4), and (5) tell how long and how fast the pony-rider worked. Choice (3) indicates that his horse was speedy to help him work fast. (Finding Topics and Main Ideas/Nonfiction)

2. **(5)** Even today five dollars would be a high price for mailing one letter. In the days of the pony-riders, it was an extremely high price. The author emphasizes the price to make it clear why *very little foolish mail was carried* (Lines 35–36). (The Author's Purpose/Nonfiction)

3. **(3)** Just as a pony-rider was *a little bit of a man* (Lines 1–2), jockeys are small. A pony-rider's clothes were *thin and fitted close* (Line 29), like a jockey's are today. The size and dress of the workers listed in the other choices are not typical of a pony-rider's. (Applying Ideas from Passages/Nonfiction)

4. **(2)** The first paragraph especially creates a sense of the great energy a pony-rider required. Pony-riders rode quickly at all times, in all weather, over all kinds of roads—even in danger. The other paragraphs support this energetic mood by describing how pony-riders did their jobs and how they and their horses were equipped for speed. (Mood and Tone/Nonfiction)

5. **(2)** The author says that the pony-rider was *full of . . . endurance* (Line 2) and that time and conditions didn't matter: *He must be always ready to leap into the saddle and be off like the wind!* (Lines 11–12). Choices (4) and (5) contradict these characteristics. Nothing is mentioned that would support Choices (1) and (3). (Inferring Ideas and Drawing Conclusions/Nonfiction)

6. **(3)** The entire passage describes some of the thoughts a father has about his relationship with his children. Although weekends, shyness, fighting, and remaining a secret are mentioned in the paragraph, each of these things is just a part of the father's thoughts. (Finding Topics and Main Ideas/Fiction)

7. **(3)** Line 6 refers to the father's work *as a disc jockey.* (Finding Details/Fiction)

8. **(4)** The father's first thoughts are about his spending time with his children, who are just 6 and 8 years old, only on weekends and Wednesday nights (see Lines 1–2). This suggests that he is divorced since someone else—probably his ex-wife—must take care of the children at other times. (Setting/Fiction)

9. **(2)** Lines 16–18 and 20–23 explain that the father fears that *they might not want to go with him next day or two nights from now or two days* if he scolds his children. (Characterization/Fiction)

10. **(4)** You learn that the father *held onto his anger* (Line 14), that he worried whether his children would want to be with him, and that although he had shown them love, they did not know each other well. The father is very concerned about the effect he has on his children. He probably considers all of his actions carefully (Characterization/Fiction)

11. **(5)** The description is in Line 1. (Finding Details/Poetry)

12. **(4)** The title mentions a guitarist. His instrument is a guitar, which can be made of wood and wires. (Inferring Unstated Details/Poetry)

13. **(4)** The word makes a connection between playing a guitar and lovers' play. (Analyzing Poetry)

14. **(2)** The first four lines describe a musician treating his guitar courteously. The last four lines compare the way he treats the guitar to the way a man treats a woman he loves. (Inferring Ideas and Drawing Conclusions/Poetry)

15. **(4)** After Picasso's study in Barcelona and Madrid, *there were no more academic tests left for him to take* (Lines 17–19). In other words, he had exhausted all the possibilities for education that Spain could offer him. (Inferring Unstated Details/Commentary)

16. **(5)** Because Picasso *could draw before he could speak* (Lines 1–2), it was clear when he was very young that he had talent. Choice (2) contradicts information in the passage. Because other artists are not mentioned in the passage, Choices (1) and (3) are not possible. The author does not suggest that Picasso didn't learn in the art schools he attended, so Choice (4) is not possible. (Inferring Ideas and Drawing Conclusions/Commentary)

17. **(2)** The paragraph is full of illustrations that demonstrate Picasso's talent. The author does not say anything that would support any of the other choices. (The Author's Purpose/Commentary)

18. **(2)** All of the other statements are facts that could be proved by school records and accounts of witnesses. Choice (2) is an opinion with which some people might disagree. (Facts and Opinions/Commentary)

19. **(5)** At the beginning of the passage, Linda is in the bedroom—perhaps she has been asleep. Willy comes home tired. In Line 47 he says *I'll start out in the morning.* All of these are clues that suggest that the passage is set at night. (Setting/Drama)

20. **(4)** When Linda says *Willy!* she expresses both a little fear (trepidation) and surprise. After Willy says *I came back,* Linda asks if something happened—as though he would not have come back if there had been nothing wrong. From these clues, you can infer that Linda knew Willy was out, but did not expect him to return so soon. (Inferring Unstated Details/Drama)

21. **(2)** All of the stage directions in the other choices show something about Linda, not Willy. (Analyzing Drama)

22. **(5)** In Lines 7–8 and 13 she simply asks whether something is wrong. In Lines 27–28 she tries to blame Willy's bad experience on the car and then (in Line 35) on his glasses. Only when she suggests that he needs a rest does she admit that something might be wrong with Willy. (Reading Dialogue/Drama)

23. **(2)** Linda is gentle and caring in everything she says to Willy. She also takes his shoes off for him (Lines 48–49) and offers to get an aspirin to soothe him. Because she seems caring, you can assume she would feed a stray animal and not chase, ignore, or abuse it. (Applying Knowledge about Characters/Drama)

Text Credits

Published by McGraw Hill Book Co. Used by permission of Raymond Carver.

65,66 Excerpt from "Keepers of the Flame" by Whitney Balliet, from *Goodbyes and Other Messages: A Journal of Jazz, 1981–1990*, Oxford University Press, 1991. Originally published in *The New Yorker*.

68 Reprinted by special permission. All rights reserved. Copyright ©1990 Bobbie Ann Mason. Originally published in *The New Yorker*.

68 Reprinted from *The American Scholar*, Volume 57, Number 2, Spring, 1988. Copyright © 1988 by the author. By permission of the publisher.

68,69 From *The Duke of Deception* by Geoffrey Wolff. Copyright © 1979 by Geoffrey Wolff. Published by Random House. Used by permission.

69 Excerpt from *The Song of Solomon* by Toni Morrison. Copyright ©1977 by Toni Morrison. Published by Alfred A. Knopf. Used by permission.

69 From *Blue Highways: A Journey into America* by William Least Heat Moon. Copyright © 1982 by William Least Heat Moon. By permission of Little, Brown and Company.

70 Excerpted from "Travels with Sukey" by Calvin Trillin from his book *Travels with Alice* published by Ticknor and Fields. Copyright © 1989 by Calvin Trillin.

70 Reprinted from *Robert Francis: Collected Poems, 1936–1976* (Amherst, University of Massachusetts, 1976). Copyright © 1936, 1964 by Robert Francis.

72,73 From *What We Talk About When We Talk About Love* by Raymond Carver. Copyright © 1981 by Raymond Carver. Reprinted by permission of Alfred A. Knopf, Inc.

74 Excerpt from *Whereabouts* by Alastair Reid. Copyright © 1990 by Alastair Reid. Published by White Pine Press. Used by permission.

75,76 From *One Man's Meat* by E. B. White. Copyright © 1944 by E. B. White. Reprinted by permission of HarperCollins Publishers.

76,77 Excerpt from "Deficits" by Michael Ignatieff. Published in *Granta 27*, Summer 1989.

78 Excerpt from *Hard to Be Good* by Bill Barich. Copyright © 1982, 1987 by Bill Barich. Reprinted by permission of Farrar, Straus & Giroux, Inc.

79 Excerpt from *Whereabouts* by Alastair Reid. Copyright © 1990 by Alastair Reid. Published by White Pine Press. Used by permission.

80,81 From *Selected Stories of Andre Dubus* by Andre Dubus. Copyright ©1988 by Andre Dubus. Published by Vintage Books. Used by permission.

82,83 From *The Glass Menagerie* by Tennessee Williams. Copyright © 1945 by Tennessee Williams and Edwina D. Williams and renewed 1973 by Tennessee Williams. Reprinted by permission of Random House.

85 Excerpt from *Hard to Be Good* by Bill Barich. Copyright © 1982, 1987 by Bill Barich. Reprinted by permission of Farrar, Straus & Giroux, Inc.

86 Excerpt from "A Memoir" by Robert Fitzgerald. Copyright ©1968 by Robert Fitzgerald. Published in *The Collected Short Prose of James Agee* by Marion Boyars Publishers, Ltd. Used by permission.

86,87 From *Selected Stories of Andre Dubus* by Andre Dubus. Copyright ©1988 by Andre Dubus. Published by Vintage Books. Used by permission.

87,88 From *The Glass Menagerie* by Tennessee Williams. Copyright © 1945 by Tennessee Williams and Edwina D. Williams and renewed 1973 by Tennessee Williams. Reprinted by permission of Random House.

89 From *The Complete Poems, 1927–1979* by Elizabeth Bishop. Copyright © 1976 by Elizabeth Bishop. Copyright © 1979, 1983 by Alice Helen Methfessel. Reprinted by permission of Farrar, Straus & Giroux.

89,90 From *The Bride and the Bachelors* by Calvin Tomkins. Copyright © 1962, 1964, 1965, 1968 by Calvin Tomkins. Used by permission of

Viking Penguin, a division of Penguin Books USA Inc. and by permission of Weidenfeld and Nicholson.

92 From the novel *Wildlife*, copyright © 1990 by Richard Ford. Reprinted with permission of Atlantic Monthly Press.

92 From *The View from 80* by Malcolm Cowley. Copyright © 1976, 1978, 1980 by Malcolm Cowley. Used by permission of Viking Penguin, a division of Penguin Books USA Inc.

93 Excerpt from *Whereabouts* by Alastair Reid. Copyright © 1990 by Alastair Reid. Published by White Pine Press. Used by permission.

96 From "The Ultimate Decision" by Andrew Malcolm. Copyright © 1989 by Andrew Malcolm. Published in *The New York Times Magazine*. December 3, 1989.

99 "Corn Pone Opinions" by Mark Twain. Published in *The Portable Mark Twain*. Copyright © 1946 by Viking Penguin, Inc., renewed 1968. Used by permission.

99 From *One Man's Meat* by E. B. White. Copyright © 1944 by E. B. White. Reprinted by permission of HarperCollins Publishers.

100,101 Excerpted from *What Are People For?* Copyright © 1990 by Wendell Berry. Published by North Point Press and reprinted by permission.

102 Excerpted from the short story "How I Met My Husband" from *Something I've Been Meaning to Tell You* by Alice Munro. Copyright ©1974 by Alice Munro. Reprinted by arrangement with Virginia Barber Literary Agency, Inc. All rights reserved.

103 Excerpt from *The Man Who Knew Too Much* by Sinclair Lewis. Copyright ©1928 by Michael Lewis. Published by Jonathan Cape Ltd./Random Century. Used by permission.

104 Excerpt from *A Good Man Is Hard to Find and Other Stories*. Copyright ©1953 by Flannery O'Connor and renewed 1981 by Mrs. Regina O'Connor, reprinted by permission of Harcourt Brace Jovanovich, Inc.

105 From *Traveling Light* by Bill Barich. Copyright © 1981, 1982, 1983, 1984 by Bill Barich. Used by permission of Viking Penguin, a division of Penguin Books USA Inc.

108 Reprinted with permission of Macmillan Publishing Company from *The Elements of Style* by William Strunk, Jr. and E. B. White.

109 Excerpted from "Full Italian Basket" by Calvin Trillin from his book *Travels with Alice* published by Ticknor and Fields. Copyright © 1989 by Calvin Trillin.

110,111 Excerpt from *The Summer Game* by Roger Angell. Copyright ©1972 by Roger Angell. Published by Viking Penguin. Used by permission.

112 From *Practicing History* by Barbara Tuchman. Copyright © 1981 by Barbara Tuchman. Reprinted by permission of Alfred A. Knopf, Inc.

114 From "Goings on About Town," January 25, 1990. Reprinted by special permission. All rights reserved. Copyright ©1990 *The New Yorker* Magazine, Inc.

116 "My Left Foot" copyright ©1989 by Pauline Kael. Originally appeared in *The New Yorker*, from *Movie Love: Complete Reviews* by Pauline Kael. Used by permission of the publisher, Dutton, an imprint of New American Library, a division of Penguin Books USA Inc.

117 Excerpt from "Getting to Know Your Synchronized Shift" by Noel Perrin. Published in the *New York Times Book Review*, December 24, 1989. Used by permission.

119 From *On the Black Hill* by Bruce Chatwin. Copyright © 1982 by Bruce Chatwin. Used by permission of Viking Penguin, a division of Penguin Books USA Inc.

120,121 Excerpt from *A Good Man Is Hard to Find and Other Stories*. Copyright ©1953 by Flannery O'Connor and renewed 1981 by Mrs. Regina O'Connor, reprinted by permission of Harcourt Brace Jovanovich, Inc.

122 Excerpt from *The Song of Solomon* by Toni Morrison. Copyright ©1977 by Toni Morrison.

Published by Alfred A Knopf. Used by permission.

123 *A Confederacy of Dunces* by John Kennedy Toole. Copyright © 1980 Thelma Toole. Published by Louisiana State University Press. Used by permission.

124,125 From *The Collected Stories of William Faulkner* by William Faulkner. Copyright © 1950 by Random House, Inc. and renewed 1977 by Jill Faulkner Summers. Reprinted by permission of the publisher and by Curtis Brown Ltd., London.

126,127 Excerpt from *The Human Comedy* by William Saroyan. Copyright © 1943 and renewed 1971 by William Saroyan, reprinted by permission of Harcourt Brace Jovanovich, Inc.

128 From *The Mosquito Coast* by Paul Theroux. Copyright © 1982 by Cape Cod Scrivners Co. Reprinted by permission of Houghton Mifflin Co. All rights reserved.

129 Excerpt from *A Good Man Is Hard to Find and Other Stories.* Copyright © 1953 by Flannery O'Connor and renewed 1981 by Mrs. Regina O'Connor, reprinted by permission of Harcourt Brace Jovanovich, Inc.

130 From *Will You Be Quiet Please?* by Raymond Carver. Copyright © 1976 by Raymond Carver. Published by McGraw Hill Book Co. Used by permission of Raymond Carver.

132,133 From *Assorted Prose* by John Updike. Copyright © 1965 by John Updike. Reprinted by permission of Alfred A. Knopf, Inc. and Andre Deutsch Ltd.

134 From *Will You Be Quiet Please?* by Raymond Carver. Copyright © 1976 by Raymond Carver. Published by McGraw Hill Book Co. Used by permission of Raymond Carver.

135,136 Excerpt from *A Yellow Raft in Blue Water* by Michael Dorris. Copyright © 1987 by Michael Dorris. Published by Warner Books, Inc. Used by permission.

137 Scene and act description from *Come Back, Little Sheba* by William Inge. Copyright © 1950 by Random House. Renewed © 1976, 1977, 1979 by Helene Connell. Used by permission.

138,139 Excerpt from NBC-TV Movie *The Old Man and the Sea* written by Roger Hirson. Based on the novella by Ernest Hemingway. Copyright © 1989 by Stoke Enterprises, Inc. Used by permission.

140,141 From *About those Roses and the Subject Was Roses* by Frank D. Gilroy. Copyright © 1965 by Frank D. Gilroy. Reprinted by permission of Random House, Inc.

142 Excerpt from *Fences* by August Wilson. Copyright © 1986 by August Wilson. Used by permission of New American Library, a division of Penguin Books USA Inc.

144 "Slipping" by Joan Aleshire. Copyright © 1983 The Modern Poetry Association. Published in *Poetry*, May 1983. Used by permission.

145,146 From *Collected Poems* by Conrad Aiken. Copyright © 1953, 1970 by Conrad Aiken, renewed 1981 by Mary Aiken. Reprinted by permission of Oxford University Press, Inc.

147 From *W. H. Auden: Collected Poems* by W. H. Auden, ed. by Edward Mendelson. Copyright © 1957 by W. H. Auden. Reprinted by permission of Random House, Inc. and by Faber and Faber Ltd.

148 "My Papa's Waltz", copyright © 1942 by Hearst Magazines, Inc. from *The Collected Poems of Theodore Roethke.* Used by permission of Doubleday, a division of Bantam Doubleday Dell Publishing Group, Inc. and by Faber and Faber Ltd.

149,150 Sonnet 130 by William Shakespeare from *The Riverside Shakespeare.* Copyright © 1974 by Houghton Mifflin Company.

151 From *Wampeters, Foma & Granfalloons* by Kurt Vonnegut Jr. Copyright © 1965, 1966, 1967, 1968, 1969, 1970, 1971, 1972, 1973, 1974 by Kurt Vonnegut Jr. Used by permission of Delacorte Press/Seymour Lawrence, a division of Bantam Doubleday Dell Publishing Group, Inc.

152 From the *Selected Stories of Andre Dubus* by Andre Dubus. Copyright © 1988 by Andre Dubus. Published by Vintage Books. Used by permission.

153 Excerpt from "Getting to Know Your Synchronized Shift" by Noel Perrin. Published in the *New York Times Book Review*, December 24, 1989. Used by permission.

153,154 "Slipping" by Joan Aleshire. Copyright © 1983 The Modern Poetry Association. Published in *Poetry*, May 1983. Used by permission.

154,155 Excerpt from NBC-TV Movie *The Old Man and the Sea* written by Roger Hirson. Based on the novella by Ernest Hemingway. Copyright © 1989 by Stoke Enterprises, Inc. Used by permission.

155,156 From *Practicing History* by Barbara Tuchman. Copyright © 1981 by Barbara Tuchman. Reprinted by permission of Alfred A. Knopf, Inc.

159 From *Toward the Radical Center: A Karel Capek Reader,* edited by Peter Kussi. Copyright © 1990 by Peter Kussi and Catbird Press. Published by Catbird Press. Used by permission.

160 Excerpt from *The Summer Game* by Roger Angell. Copyright © 1972 by Roger Angell. Published by Viking Penguin. Used by permission.

160 *Poems of W. B. Yeats* edited by Richard J. Finneran. Copyright © 1934 by Macmillan Publishing Company, renewed 1962 by Bertha Georgie Yeats.

164 From *Roughing It* by Mark Twain published by Viking Press. Used by permission.

165 From the *Selected Stories of Andre Dubus* by Andre Dubus. Copyright © 1988 by Andre Dubus. Published by Vintage Books. Used by permission.

166 "The Guitarist Tunes Up" by Frances Cornford. Used by permission of Random Century.

166 Excerpt from *The Success and Failure of Picasso* by John Berger. Copyright © 1965 by John Berger. Published by Pantheon Books.

167 From *Death of a Salesman* by Arthur Miller. Copyright © 1949, renewed © 1977, by Arthur Miller. Used by permission of Viking Penguin, a division of Penguin Books USA Inc.

Illustrations

Page	Credit
1	New York Zoological Society Photo
9	AP/Worldwide Photos
13	Courtesy of Museum of the American Indian/Heye Foundation
19	Courtesy of The American Museum of Natural History
25	International Newsreel
33	Library of Congress, Dorothea Lange
38	Joseph Smith Historic Center—Joseph Smith Homestead
55	David Rees. Copyright © 1991
65	Greater New Orleans Tourist and Convention Commission
75	U.S. Department of the Interior
95	AP/Worldwide Photos
98	Stan Wakefield
111	Ken Karp
125	Kosti Ruohomaa/Black Star
131	Irene Springer
156	Marc P. Anderson
163	Hurok Productions

The editors have made every effort to trace the ownership of all copyrighted material and express regret in advance for any error or omission. After notification of an oversight, they will include proper acknowledgement in future printings.